REMEMBERING

CRAWFORD COUNTY

REMEMBERING

CRAWFORD COUNTY

PENNSYLVANIA'S LAST FRONTIER

ROBERT D. ILISEVICH

Charleston · London

THE
History
PRESS

Published by The History Press
Charleston, SC 29403
www.historypress.net

First published 2008

Manufactured in the United States

ISBN 978.1.59629.570.4

Library of Congress Cataloging-in-Publication Data

Ilisevich, Robert D.
Remembering Crawford County : Pennsylvania's last frontier / Robert D. Ilisevich.
p. cm.
ISBN 978-1-59629-570-4
1. Crawford County (Pa.)--History. 2. Frontier and pioneer life--Pennsylvania--Crawford
County. 3. Crawford County (Pa.)--Politics and government. 4. Crawford County (Pa.)--
Biography. 5. Crawford County (Pa.)--Social conditions. I. Title.
F157.C77I455 2008
974.8'97--dc22
                              2008037210

CONTENTS

CONTENTS

PREFACE

This is not a traditional history book. Structurally, it defies chronology, lacks a directional pointer and is devoid of footnotes and bibliography. Simply, it is a set of essays about interesting persons and episodes in two hundred years of Crawford County history. A number of these writings have previously appeared in the *Meadville Tribune* and the Crawford County Historical Society newsletter, and have been edited for this publication.

Subjects and accompanying events were chosen for their contribution to a better understanding of the county's past. With only twenty-eight essays, a wider selection was out of the question. Thus, many equally important subjects did not make the final cut. A partial list of these includes churches, sports, fraternals and unions, minorities, military and the environment. No effort was made to discriminate against the selection of any of these.

Hopefully, each of the following essays will raise questions and lead to additional investigation and fresh interpretation. Constant revisionism is what makes the study of history move forward.

If there is a theme in these essays, it is the individual with leadership qualities who resolved problems or prevented some from even happening. There was not a single group, class or particular part of the county that produced this kind of individual. He could have been a businessman, farmer, educator, writer, politician, inventor or just a dreamer. All of these appear in the essays. Collectively, they committed themselves to advancing the community from one generation to the next, from frontier days to the computer age.

PREFACE

I am first indebted to those past local historians who not only wrote of their times, but who also were mindful of the fact that without source materials there can be no history. They labored to collect and preserve manuscripts, photographs, newspapers and maps to enable future historians to examine the past better.

Second, I am grateful to the Crawford County Historical Society for allowing me free access to its wonderful collection—one of the finest in the commonwealth—and permitting the use of its staff and office hardware.

Third, special thanks go to a group of four, without whom this work would not have been possible. Anne Stewart, who knows more about Meadville history than anyone I know, consistently assisted me and helped select special photographs. Also helping to obtain the more difficult finds was Larry Wonders, who has inventoried thousands of the society's photographs and knows exactly where they are located. Without Kevin Pipp, the rest of us would have been at a loss to scan images and work with the editor on the technical side of publishing. And full credit for typing, editing and formatting the manuscript has to go to Natalie Kelley-Wilson, who understands and applies the growing wonders of the computer.

Finally, a nod of appreciation goes to Jonathan Simcosky, Jaime Muehl and the editorial staff at The History Press for doing what was necessary to produce the finished product and to the *Meadville Tribune* for permitting the republishing of some of the essays.

LOOKING AT CRAWFORD COUNTY

In May 1788, David Mead, leading a small band of future settlers to their new home in Northwest Pennsylvania, knew, along with the others, that the problems they were about to face were strong enough to cause the men to turn back. Their destination was the former native village of Cussewago that stood on the southwest shore of the creek of the same name. They conjured up troubling memories of struggling with previous frontiers back east. They hoped that this frontier—Pennsylvania's last—would not be as bad. After all, they planned to bring their families out here once initial settlement had been made.

Mead must have known of George Washington's report to Governor Robert Dinwiddie of Virginia, submitted after he had made his famous journey to this part of Pennsylvania in 1753 to inform the French that they were on Virginia soil. Washington wrote of traveling over "much good land...extensive and very rich meadows, one of which I believe was nearly four miles in length." Then again, Mead may have learned of General William Irvine's 1785 exploratory report of the same region, in which he also spoke of the good land.

Mead was personally familiar with the area to which his party was heading. In the previous year, he and his brother John had explored the flats around the confluence of the Cussewago with French Creek. Apparently the grass-covered fields they found had been previously cultivated by either an earlier native culture or the French.

The nagging question that haunted everyone in Mead's party focused on the Native Americans they anticipated finding in the area. Since the Revolutionary War, the national government had tried to resolve differences with Western tribes regarding future white settlements in the Ohio country. The white man's diplomacy failed when some of the tribes, including the Miami and Shawnee, insisted on the Ohio River as the undisputed boundary.

The Seneca, the largest and westernmost tribe of the Iroquois Confederacy, opposed any plan that might lead to war. The Seneca essentially controlled French Creek Valley. Its local chief, Cornplanter, whose people lived in the upper reaches of the Allegheny River, eventually befriended Mead's settlers and hoped to arrange with the national government certain benefits for his people. Could this powerful chief possibly keep the Western tribes in check with this kind of diplomacy? Mead's people hoped so.

Closely akin to the potentially hostile western tribes were those tribes along the Canadian border that had supported the British during the Revolutionary War. They were becoming increasingly restless because they stood between the Americans, who didn't care to have anything to do with them, and the British, whose support had dwindled once the war had ended. Unfortunately for all concerned, with peace restored, not all of the issues—particularly that of the Northwest posts—had been satisfactorily resolved. What this meant to Mead's party was the horrible prospect of restless tribes suddenly becoming hostile as well.

Finally, Mead was aware of the growing land problem in the northwestern region of Pennsylvania. Actually, it became the biggest ongoing headache for settlers in the two decades following the 1788 settlement. Conflicting claims were at the heart of the problem. Mead and his party had experienced this kind of conflict back in Northumberland County—a conflict between Connecticut and Pennsylvania over lands in the Wyoming Valley. Mead and others had lost in that legal battle. Pennsylvania compensated some settlers for their losses. Nearly eight years after he had settled at Cussewago, Mead also received compensation with "Wyoming credits" that entitled him to receive four hundred acres along Sandy Creek, miles south of his settlement.

Title disputes in what became Crawford County erupted between those who had a legitimate claim and those who did not. Veterans of the Revolutionary War who had received donation tracts and land companies that had received hundreds of thousands of acres from the state held legal claims. Those without them were generally called squatters. Some, like Mead, who made improvements as required by law and filed for title under preemption, were not the problem. Instead, it was the squatter who knew he was on somebody's tract, but settled anyway because no one occupied it. He argued that, since the tract showed no signs of having been improved, it became available to others. Some won their cases; others were evicted.

The early days of Mead's settlement tested the will and resourcefulness of the pioneers. As feared, trouble occurred with the natives, but it was not with the locals like the Mohawk chief, Stripe Neck, and the sons of Chief Canadaughta, Flying Cloud, Big Sun and Standing Stone. As expected, the threat came from the West. Encouraged by their crushing victory over General Hosiah Harmar in 1790, these Western tribes decided to snuff out all settlements west of the Allegheny River and north of the Ohio.

Mead evacuated his people to the safety of Fort Franklin, some thirty miles to the south. Chief Halftown and his warriors guarded the fleeing party from possible ambush. Cornplanter pledged to make peace with the warring tribes, but it was General Anthony Wayne's defeat of the tribes in 1794 at Fallen Timbers that temporarily restored peace, after a few settlers had been killed.

Crawford County was established in 1800 with the break up of the large Federalist county of Allegheny following the victory of the Democratic Republicans and the 1799 election of Thomas McKean as governor. Six other western counties were established at this time, thus increasing the number of county officials the new governor could appoint. Meadville became the county seat with a court of common pleas that had jurisdiction over the new counties of Warren, Venango, Erie and Mercer. The first president judge was Alexander Addison; associate judges were David Mead and John Kelso. Meadville suddenly became a Mecca of practicing attorneys.

Meadville was also a Federalist stronghold in northwestern Pennsylvania. The surrounding townships and adjacent counties were Republican. Political division became a permanent reality in the county—Federalists v. Republicans, Whigs v. Democrats and Democrats v. Republicans. The partisanship was so robust in the early years that even social gatherings were arranged according to political sentiments.

During the first half of the nineteenth century, the county grew with an economy balanced between agriculture and an assortment of small businesses. Improved roads and accommodating waterways, including the canal, aided the commercial interests. Land companies were important in the county's economic development, for they brought in settlers and helped them by providing mills and roads, tools and livestock. They imported Eastern capitalism into a frontier economy that had essentially functioned on the practice of carrying on trade by bartering.

By the time of the Civil War, manufacturing was increasing, the oil industry was booming after Edwin Drake's successful oil probe in 1859 near Titusville and the railroad was inching closer to the county line. In November 1862, the rails finally reached Meadville. It took only a few years and three major events—the coming of the railroad, the oil boom and the war—to revolutionize Crawford County's economy.

Each of these events had to have support industries. Meadville and Titusville assumed most of the responsibility of constructing factories to turn out such products as barrels, tools and machine parts. Because of the war's drain on manpower, immigrants had to be employed. Many of these were Irish and Swedes who helped complete the Atlantic & Great Western Railroad through the county. It was then possible to ride the six-foot-gauge train east to New York City and west to the Mississippi.

In the years since the Civil War, the pattern of county life revealed the deepening impress of the city. Urban pressures born of the Industrial Revolution swept away any remaining vestiges of the frontier and acted as a magnet in drawing rural folk and immigrants to Meadville and Titusville or large towns outside the county. They went to these towns because the jobs were there.

Toolmaking became and remained the signature of county manufacturing, while unique industries producing stereoscopic equipment, zippers and corsets attained national and international recognition. In a diverse agricultural system, stock breeding, especially of horses, received worldwide fame until the gasoline engine dampened the market. Servicing all these factories and businesses were additional women, immigrants and minorities, who considerably strengthened the economic progress being made.

The economic gains helped nourish both traditional and pop cultures. A generation after its founding, Meadville had already been recognized as the center of enlightenment for all Northwest Pennsylvania. The town boasted of having schools, an academy, a college (Allegheny), churches, private libraries and one of the first newspapers west of the Alleghenies, the *Crawford Weekly Messenger*.

This strong tradition of learning continued through the remainder of the nineteenth century and into the twentieth. A big role was played by a number of literary, library, scientific and thespian organizations, as well as publications like *The Chautauquan*. In addition, the newspaper continued to be the medium most county residents enjoyed reading for the latest news. At the turn of the twentieth century, at least a half dozen daily and weekly papers were published throughout the county.

Then there was the pop culture, sometimes called "mass culture" due to its appeal to urban masses. Easily affordable, generally lowbrow and delightfully enjoyable, these included sports, the circus and cheap theaters featuring vaudeville shows or motion pictures. They grew rapidly. Debate often raged between custodians of classical learning and the supporters of this light entertainment. Because agreement could never occur, it had to give way to compromise. Children could still see a circus and watch movies, but they also had to attend concerts and read the classics. The academic, at the same time, could take in ballgames and attend slapstick comedies. No argument ensued when it came to attending the county fair, one of the larger and more successful fairs throughout the commonwealth. Everyone looked forward to attending this annual event.

Also on the light side were family recreational facilities. Conneaut Lake and Exposition Park became instantly popular. The train and trolley brought in thousands of visitors, some from distant cities like Pittsburgh and Cleveland. After the park had added a hotel, carousel, thrill rides and a dance hall, popularity increased. Soon, other communities, like Meadville and Cambridge Springs, built picnic groves and amusement parks. When both the commonwealth and the county became seriously concerned with flooding in French Creek Valley, Pymatuning Spillway and Woodcock Lake were created to hold back the waters. In recent years, boating, fishing and swimming in these waters have been exceedingly attractive.

In a little more than two centuries, Crawford County has gone from being a frontier settlement to a community of modern factories, farms, hospitals and colleges, with a growing population of mixed races, nationalities and religions. Its beautiful streams, hills, parks, institutions and recreational areas attract people from everywhere. Researchers, especially genealogists, find the county's resources to be among the best in the commonwealth.

Aside from Meadville and Titusville, the county towns are small, yet characteristically distinctive because of their histories, traditions and people. In its pioneer days, the county occupied a strategic position in the communication and trade network between the Great Lakes and the Ohio Valley. Today, it is approximately equidistant to Pittsburgh, Cleveland and Buffalo. Just as geography had an impact on its importance in the beginning, so the county's location today enables it to play an equally important role.

COUNTY'S LAST "DUEL IN THE SUN"

Presumably, it was the last recorded duel in Crawford County, and undoubtedly it occurred in broad daylight. Duelists were notoriously bad shots. Even with plenty of light, they often missed each other. Sometimes, in their agitated states of mind, they would try and try again until one of them was hit.

The county duelists were land agent Roger Alden and attorney Alexander Foster. We're not sure why these leading citizens wanted to kill each other, but a woman may have been the reason. In 1804, they rendezvoused on the bank of French Creek just south of Meadville. Alden got shot in the leg, either above or below the knee. Sources can't seem to agree.

At least the combatants were smart enough to have surgeons for their seconds—Dr. Kennedy of Meadville for Alden and Dr. Wallace of Erie for Foster. Alden allegedly refused to admit defeat and instead wanted another crack at Foster, but the seconds ruled against it. He may have been lame afterward, but according to newspaperman J.C. Hays, "He gained the lady in question."

Dueling dates back to feudal times, perhaps as a development of chivalry. With its code and set procedure, it sprang from the idea of protecting one's honor. For centuries, both the monarchy and the Church were inconsistent on the question of whether killing of this nature was ever justified. Cynics decried every effort to justify what was to them ordinary murder. As constitutional and judicial systems evolved, written law came to protect against defamatory statements designed to injure one's reputation, but dueling continued.

Roger Alden. *Crawford County Historical Society.*

In time, this grizzly game of gunplay worked its way to America. If English gentlemen like William Pitt and Lord Byron could do it, why not the class-conscious Brahmins of Boston and Philadelphia? The most famous duel in this country occurred between political rivals Vice President Aaron Burr and Alexander Hamilton. Burr challenged Hamilton, who hesitated to accept at first, but then decided to go through with it. He had lost a son in a duel. One version of what happened had Hamilton firing deliberately over Burr's head. The vice president, however, took careful aim and mortally wounded Hamilton.

Closer to home, debonair Tarleton Bates of Pittsburgh, who had been maligned by Ephraim Pentland, a highly critical editor, refused to issue a challenge because Pentland was not a social equal (a curious condition of the sport). Instead, he gave the editor a horsewhipping on a city street. Pentland then sent, through his merchant friend, Thomas Stewart, a challenge to Bates, who explained in a newspaper article why he could not accept. Taking offense to something that Bates had written about him, Stewart challenged Bates, who this time accepted. Stewart may have been to Bates a scoundrel and lackey, but he was still socially acceptable for a challenge! In what became the Oakland section of the city, Stewart proved to be a better shot than Bates, who was killed.

A good friend of Bates, Henry Baldwin (builder of the Baldwin-Reynolds House), also engaged in a Pittsburgh duel, at least according to an early historian. It nearly cost him his life, which was spared when the bullet hit a silver dollar in his vest pocket. True or not, it is an odd but interesting story that impressed Robert Ripley enough to publish it in his *Believe It Or Not!*

By the time dueling reached the Mississippi Valley, it had been Americanized by the frontier. While it retained the idea of killing, the Western duel undid the niceties. The exchange of formal notes and the use of seconds had become passé. Along with spectators who loved the action, an undertaker, doctor or sheriff might witness the spectacle. Traditionally, the winner walked away, free from the law as long as the duel was not illegal. Foster and Stewart walked away. Burr temporarily fled authorities, but then returned to Washington to resume his official duties.

Over the decades, storytellers have glamorized the violence of men killing men according to the Code of the West—protecting one's honor, women and property. While lawmen like Wyatt Earp and "Bat" Masterson were cleansing cattle and mining towns of gun-happy rabble, expert gunslingers were gaining notoriety. Yet they lived in constant danger of being goaded into drawing by some upstart who wanted instant glory and the reputation of being the "fastest gun west of the Pecos." Most challengers only landed on Boot Hill.

The movies and television have made their share of frontier heroes. For years, TV's Marshal Dillon of *Gunsmoke* killed scores of bad men, but always in an acceptable manner. Anything was acceptable because Dillon typified all the good qualities of the Westerner. At fifty paces he never missed, and his audiences applauded. A Clint Eastwood movie character, in contrast, could down three outlaws at once by shooting from the hip. Exaggerating the facts to make a real or fictional figure bigger than big is something movie and television directors love to do. It is no way to teach history, admittedly, but who cares? As long as good triumphs over evil, the audience is satisfied and the historian is muted.

The Western shootout was truly a caricature of the centuries-old duel, with its traditions that no participating gentleman dared violate. Just as the frontier tended to obliterate class distinctions, so the six-shooter, it was said, equalized everyone. If the frontier embodied democratic spirit, as many historians believe it did, then it had to include the inane "quick draw" and killing. When the frontier came to an end, so did its heroes. Yet our perception of them, right or wrong, remains, whether it be of Earp, Dillon or some villainous gunslinger with twenty or so dead challengers on his resume.

EARLY LAND BARONS
OF CRAWFORD COUNTY

Writing in 1876, Alfred Huidekoper tried to distinguish between "good and bad" land speculators. He was making particular references to the Holland Land Company, which, in his opinion, had conducted its operations in a most honorable manner. Perhaps he was just defending his father, Harm Jan Huidekoper, who for many years as the company's agent in Meadville had amassed a great fortune. Maybe his father needed defending; maybe he didn't.

The basis of Harm's wealth was land. With others, he found the virgin forests and fields of Crawford County and surrounding counties an exciting place for investment. Some, like Harm, became permanent residents and helped build new communities. Others were transients or absentee landlords who merely sought quick profits from the nation's most abundant commodity. Together they made up a class of land barons who played a big part in the history of Northwest Pennsylvania.

When Harm first visited the county in 1802, he noticed two things immediately: one was the abject poverty and the other was the total confusion in land ownership. The tax records of 1800 show that many of the first settlers had large tracts—the average being about four hundred acres—but very little else. Of the 280 or so heads of families who had farms in Mead Township, 117 had neither horse nor oxen to work the land. They were poor, and in many instances, the soil they occupied was poor.

Moreover, many of them were deeply involved in legal squabbles over land titles. The Pennsylvania Land Law of 1792 was so loosely worded that even the courts could not agree upon an interpretation. The law's vagueness was intentionally inserted by legislators who backed the speculator, thus making this part of the state a happy hunting ground for land jobbers.

What assisted them was the fact that many warrant holders had deserted their farms in the face of the Indian uprising in the early 1790s. Therefore, they could not technically comply with the law's residency requirement of two years. The deserted lands were then seized and claimed by "squatters," or intruders, who refused to recognize the rights of the original owners if and when they returned. Many intruders were just unwary dupes of unscrupulous jobbers who pocketed extra money by leading innocent settlers to the vacated tracts. Since much of this land had been originally contracted by the Holland Land Company, Huidekoper declared war on the trespassers. The whole thing got pretty messy. In 1805, the United States Supreme Court, in *Huidekoper's Lessee v. Douglass*, ruled in favor of the original owners or warrantees. By this time, the typical settler had been turned off by land agents, good or bad.

Some took advantage of this sordid situation. Roger Alden, Huidekoper's predecessor, saw fortune, fame and social honors come quickly his way. As agent, he was in the position to bid upon some of the best real estate available. By the time he was replaced by Huidekoper, who did not think very much of him as a businessman, Alden had acquired over one thousand acres plus 31 lots in Mead Township alone. And that was not all. The tax records of 1805 also show that Alden and his business partner, Dr. Thomas Kennedy, had picked up more than 130 city lots and out-lots and over three hundred acres in the same township.

Alden's contributions to the community were never measured in terms of the land he possessed. Instead, he is best remembered for his many civic accomplishments, including his plan of 1795 for downtown Meadville. Actually, he had overspeculated in land and found that he couldn't pay all his taxes. When he left here in 1827 to become quartermaster at West Point, his financial position had deteriorated considerably. In fact, he couldn't afford to take his family to the Point. Meanwhile, his partner was becoming richer with each passing day.

Early in his medical career, Kennedy had discovered that caring for patients over a large stretch of Northwest Pennsylvania was neither physically nor financially rewarding. Therefore, he decided to turn his

Dr. Thomas Kennedy. *Crawford County Historical Society.*

practice over to another young and promising physician, Daniel Bemus, so that he might devote his time, energy and resources to various business adventures, including land investments. At the time of his death in 1813, Kennedy owned sizable properties in Crawford, Erie, Mercer, Venango, Chester and Warren Counties. Furthermore, he had purchased some three thousand acres in Western New York, where he had established a lumber business. Incidentally, Dr. Bemus also looked beyond medicine for financial security. He dabbled in land, lumber and oil and died a very rich man.

When it came to owning land, however, no one came close to Harm Huidekoper. It is nearly impossible to assess his total holdings or worth at any point in time before his death. Like Alden, this Hollander used his position as agent to acquire choice properties. The thousands of acres that he acquired or controlled was a tribute not only to his enterprising abilities, but also to the awful land system that prevailed during the first decades of the county's history. Both federal and state governments promoted policies that allowed those with capital to buy as much as they wanted at prices low enough for the speculator but generally too high for the actual settler. It is little wonder that, by the 1840s, many social and land reformers were demanding that the government adopt a homestead bill that would give free land to the bona fide settler and lower the boom on the speculator.

Huidekoper's enormous land investments put him into a class reserved for a special few, like Jared Shattuck, a Connecticut Yankee who had become a successful merchant prior to his arrival in Meadville in 1817. He and his partner, Gad Peck, purchased some ninety thousand acres in this part of the country for $160,000. By then, the land fever had reached a new high; the westward push had exceeded all expectations. Shattuck's sales soared to something like $100,000 in no time at all, but so destitute were the settlers who occupied his lands that he could hardly collect enough from them to pay taxes on his remaining tracts. When interest alone on his debts climbed to over $50,000, Shattuck realized that it was time to get out. He liquidated most of his holdings. Peck had bowed out earlier and had moved to Ohio.

Shattuck and Peck were not the only ones who found their adventure in land speculation frustrating. Henry Baldwin and Stephen Barlow were another pair who came up short. In 1816, they purchased some 250,000 acres for about $90,000 at a time when the market was glutted. They lost heavily when they failed on their loans. Baldwin's huge losses plagued him for the rest of his life.

Also joining the list of losers were federal judge William Griffith of New Jersey and attorney J.B. Wallace of Philadelphia. They acquired some one thousand shares of the Pennsylvania Population Company before it dissolved in 1812. About the same time, the two men bought tracts from the Holland Land Company, but the company retained certain control of management. The tracts were essentially in Crawford and Erie Counties. Griffith and Wallace put the land under the care of Huidekoper and hired Augustus Sacket and William Hart as agents to make actual sales to settlers. Huidekoper referred to Sacket as a man "without principles, morals or talents." Free-swinging deals by these agents ended in disaster. Many of their transactions were mere "paper sales" when purchasers failed to meet their financial obligations. Wallace eventually moved to Meadville, where he disposed of his holdings. In 1836, Huidekoper picked up the last of Wallace's holdings, an estimated 58,300 acres, for which he and his sons paid the Holland Land Company $178,400.

Less notorious than Alden, Kennedy, Huidekoper, Shattuck and Wallace were those early landowners who neither owned nor speculated as much and who are best associated with township histories. One of these was Jacob Guy, who came early to what became Randolph Township and shortly accumulated several thousand acres. Ebenezer Felton started out as a land agent, and he, too, acquired substantial acreage throughout the county. The ledger entitled "Treasurer's Sales of Unseated Lands for Crawford County for the years 1816 to 1846" shows precisely those who constantly were in and out of the land market, picking up bargains for payment of delinquent taxes. Some of the county's leading citizens were involved: John Reynolds, Ward Barney, Thomas Atkinson, William Magaw, Arthur Cullum, J. Stuart Riddle and Conner Clark. There were many others.

Generally, we think of these men as businesspeople, lawyers, printers, etc., and not as land speculators. But dabbling in land was an integral part of the Western mind. To some, it became a disease, the first step toward power, prestige and wealth. They had migrated from the East with a strong realization that many fortunes back there, like that of the Astors, had been the result of successful land manipulation. But we'll never know what percentage of those who made their way across the mountains were only motivated by a greed to grab as much as they could and how many came simply to settle upon a small tract and raise a family.

The land baron was actually speculating on the country's progress. He knew he could count upon future pressures for more land as the westward movement intensified after 1800, made easy by the increasing liberality of federal land policies. Values just had to go up. Regrettably, this attitude was passed on to the poor pioneers, who saw that they, too, could keep moving deeper into the West, always selling their lands for a profit after making minimal improvements. The turnover of settlers was often high in some communities. This was demoralizing to those who wanted more permanency in their towns and townships. But the frontiersman had a migratory itch that broke down local attachments and discouraged intensive improvements.

This compulsive tendency to move on must not be used as a general indictment against our first settlers. The irresistible urge to exploit the land, especially since there was so much of it, seemed such a natural thing to do. Again, many came to stay. Their commitment to their families and communities was stronger than any desire to make a fast buck, pull up stakes and move on. For those who did acquire fortune and social respectability from their land dealings, it should be pointed out that they often achieved this at the cost of general community development. Their obsession with land acquisition often blinded them to those economic areas that needed strengthening. In 1807, Roger Alden spoke of three dangers to the local economy: the scarcity of specie, the want of manufacturing and the high cost of transportation. Forty years later, a number of angry citizens complained of the same things, in addition to falling land values and a generally depressed economy. Some of these settlers would soon leave Crawford County for greener pastures. For this, the early land barons must accept some responsibility.

PERRY'S HELPMATES

County Contributed to 1813 Lake Erie Victory

On September 10, 1813, Oliver Hazard Perry's American squadron defeated the British on Lake Erie. In 2003, as we celebrated the 190th anniversary of this remarkable victory, we reminded ourselves of Crawford County's contributions.

While local farmers and merchants provided food and supplies, men joined the ranks, and Meadville hosted military companies from the western and central regions of the commonwealth. But it was the unique role that some Crawford Countians played in readying the American squadron for action that deserves special attention.

The War of 1812 was not one of America's better organized and executed adventures. Neither President James Madison nor his generals demonstrated any talent for military planning. In addition, many Americans opposed the war. With the nation so divided against itself and ill prepared, the first year of the war could not miss being a disaster.

Probably the worst place for an American to be in the spring of 1812 was anywhere along the Canadian border. The British controlled the lakes, and reports from lakefront settlements told of huge quantities of guns and supplies being distributed from British forts to native tribes. New fears led to chilling stories of burning cabins and screaming victims of Indian brutalities. The great Shawnee Chief Tecumseh promised revenge for the humiliation suffered the previous year at the Battle of Tippecanoe.

The surrender of Detroit and Fort Michilimackinac created panic across northwestern Pennsylvania. Daniel Dobbins of Erie, who had

Thomas Atkinson. *Crawford County Historical Society.*

escaped from his British captors, convinced the Madison administration that a squadron should be built at Erie to fend off enemy warships and landing parties. After painstaking efforts against haughty superiors and shortages of every kind, he managed to oversee the construction of several warships and to assemble a squadron of eleven vessels.

Dobbins decided to build the ships in the bay. Sheltered by Presque Isle and a sandbar that guarded the entrance to the bay, the squadron was protected from enemy attack. Only local pilots familiar with the channel over the sandbar would attempt to enter the bay. The British commander, Robert Barclay, boasted of how he would demolish the American ships as they ran aground on the sandbar. If British warships could not enter the bay, he argued, the American ships would not leave their sanctuary.

Barclay had a point. By the end of July, the water over the sandbar was much too shallow for the brigs under construction, the *Niagara* and the *Lawrence*, each with a draft of nine feet. Yet the ingenious Dobbins and his crew had anticipated the problem and had a plan ready when it was time to take the ships into the lake.

The time arrived when several enemy warships passed near the entrance to the bay. Perry believed that an invading force was at hand and immediately appealed to General David Mead for help. On July 21, in the *Crawford Weekly Messenger*, Mead made an emotional plea: "Citizens to Arms! Your state is invaded. The enemy has arrived at Erie threatening to destroy our navy and town…"

Public response exceeded expectations. Many men, young and old, took up their muskets and headed north. Even the *Messenger*'s owner/editor, Thomas Atkinson, suspended operations and joined the march.

To the surprise of the volunteers, there was no invading force, and the enemy ships were gone. It was rumored that Barclay had pulled back in order to attend a dinner in his honor at Port Dover. Apparently, he was confident that the American ships would not attempt to leave the harbor before he returned. This miscalculation of Barclay's was the break Perry, Dobbins, Mead and others needed.

They now hurried to raise the vessels over the sandbar by the use of four "camels." A camel was a watertight structure—fifty feet long, ten feet wide and eight feet deep—so built that water could be let in or pumped out. The camels were placed on each side of the vessel and filled with water; long timbers with ends resting on the camels were thrust through the gun ports (the cannon and rigging had been removed to reduce the weight of the vessel).

As the water was pumped out of the camels, the vessel rose. Mead's men then helped push and pull the vessel across the sandbar. It was a slow procedure that had to be repeated a number of times. Only after a two-day struggle did the men succeed in getting the *Lawrence* across the sandbar. Other vessels followed.

The mission was accomplished. The squadron entered the lake and began its search for the enemy. In several weeks, the historic battle took place.

Perry thanked Mead and his men for their assistance. He was also grateful for the volunteers who accompanied him in search of the enemy. Meadville's Harm Huidekoper estimated that seventy-two men who went with Perry were from the county. And nobody celebrated Perry's victory more than the citizens of Crawford County. They were especially proud of the role they had played.

EARLY POLITICS NEARLY LED
TO A MEADVILLE RIOT

Nobody loves a riot. Whether it springs from a soccer game or results from a clash between strikebreakers and union workers, the specter of men hurling themselves at one another chills any community. In less than two decades after its founding, Meadville experienced what almost became its first full-scale riot.

The politics of Crawford County in the first decade of the nineteenth century were divisive and crude. Federalists and Republicans battled over land issues, internal improvements and banks. There was little they didn't fight over. Writing to Thomas Jefferson in 1806, Patrick Farrelly, prominent Meadville attorney, intimidated local Federalists when he accused them of being unfriendly to the national government for taking part in a clandestine operation that became known as the "Burr Conspiracy." His remarks were to the point but mild. Other Republicans branded the Burr supporters as traitors and asked for their heads. Whether it was a conspiracy to commit treason against the United States is no longer a pressing issue. Any viewpoint can be defended. Of greater interest is the story of those people from Crawford County whose lives and careers were affected by the episode.

Aaron Burr's own political career was brilliant but warped by imaginative grasps for power and glory. Rejected for the vice presidency by Jefferson in 1804, Burr decided to run for governor of New York with a strong promise of Federalist support. But his efforts were frustrated by his chief New York rival, Alexander Hamilton. So bitter were the invectives between the two men that a duel ensued. When Burr killed

Hamilton, a young nation was stunned. With one fatal shot, Burr had forfeited all rights to any political ambition he may have had. Yet he was not through.

He fled west to avoid arrest and to exploit two dominant forces in the country at that time: expansionism and separatism. His exact plans seemed vague and contradictory; perhaps Burr himself was no more sure of them than is the historian today. Evidence suggests that he expected to be offered the presidency of New Orleans when it declared its independence from the Union. The next move might then be a war against Spain—a conflict that would be popular with many Westerners—with Burr himself possibly leading the revolution in Mexico. The end result would be a new empire carved from Spanish-held territory, with Burr at its head.

However fantastic and incredulous the scheme may have been, the fact that many prominent men in the West attached themselves to it, and the fact that there was something mysterious about it, created a furor in the entire country on this side of the mountains. Burr's appeal seemed magnetic. Thousands of men pledged their support to him. Writing from Pittsburgh in December 1806, Fredrick Bates reported that Burr's plans seemed complete and that many young men of education and wealth were descending the river. Burr's agents had succeeded in selling a dreamy adventure to a bunch of starry-eyed pioneers.

In his letter to the president, Farrelly mentioned two of these agents, Captain Davis and Colonel Smith, who came to Crawford County with offers tempting to anyone who wanted to listen. By November 24, 1806, nine men, again according to Farrelly, had been recruited, and on that day they departed in canoes for Beaver Creek, the place of rendezvous on the Ohio, to join the expeditionary force. Eight names of the nine are legible in Farrelly's letter. They include Frederick Haymaker, Luke Hill, Hugh Allen, James Kennedy Carpenter, Owen Aston, William Davis and two chaps by the names of Burnside and Chidester. There may have been others, but the historical evidence is lacking.

What reasons motivated these men to leave their families and friends for some unknown destiny we'll never know. Farrelly called them Federalists and claimed that some of them were fleeing their creditors. This may have been the case with Luke Hill, the legendary boatman and merchant who did go bankrupt. But insolvency was probably not that significant a factor. On the other hand, we cannot be sure that politics was the reason either. Most likely, some combination of adventure, fame and fortune prompted these men to take the long boat ride south.

Some returned; some didn't. Some met tragedy; others returned to resume a normal life or, as the editor of the *Crawford Weekly Messenger*, Thomas Atkinson, cynically called it: "the dull pursuits of civil life." Luke Hill disappeared somewhere in Louisiana. William Davis, a promising talent in the prothonotary's office, never found his El Dorado. His premature death in 1809 at Natchez, Mississippi, shocked his many friends back home. The tragedy was compounded when it was learned that his sister, Rachel, who had married another one of the nine— Frederick Haymaker—had died in childbirth about the same time. Family records indicate that Haymaker, former merchant, postmaster and justice of the peace, served as Burr's personal secretary. He never returned to Crawford County.

Then there is Burnside, presumably William Burnside, the brawny blacksmith of Pine Township, who returned and changed his politics, who later dropped everything to join Mead and others to fight in the War of 1812 and who was eventually murdered near his home.

Getting back to Atkinson, he was the fiery newspaperman who, in 1805, started the first paper in town. Over the years, he had several partners who helped with the paper, including the future fifteenth president of the United States, James Buchanan, who made frequent trips to Meadville to visit his sister. In addition to putting out a weekly, Atkinson became one of the town's leading citizens, serving as burgess, county commissioner, first secretary of the chamber of commerce and elected representative to the state legislature. When David Mead gathered a company of locals and marched them to Erie to defend against the British in the War of 1812, Atkinson stopped the press, picked up his rifle and joined Mead.

Atkinson had no doubts regarding his position in the sordid Burr affair. He pointed an accusing finger at Jabez Colt, agent for the Pennsylvania Population Company, who befriended Captain Davis, Burr's emissary in this region. It was Colt who recommended Hugh Allen to Davis, who then introduced him to Comfort Tyler, one of Burr's principal agents. Furthermore, Atkinson charged Colt with malicious intent of joining the expedition himself until his "cowardly heart failed" upon hearing of Jefferson's plan of reprisal against the conspirators. Atkinson was sure

Pieter Huidekoper, younger brother of Harm J. Huidekoper. *Crawford County Historical Society.*

that Colt knew of and undoubtedly encouraged the financial backing that some men of Meadville were providing for the adventure. As a footnote, Burr had been one of the chief backers of the Pennsylvania Population Company, a land outfit that speculated heavily in lands in this part of the state.

Atkinson's free-swinging journalism couldn't help but affirm polarity of political sentiment in the community. Colt, Federalists, Pennsylvania Population Company, Burr—all together in a cause that smacked of treason! A man of Atkinson's editorial talents couldn't ask for a better setup. By implicating Colt and his Federalist friends, Atkinson had succeeded in rallying support from his Republican readers against two long-standing enemies of the poor settler: the land speculator and the rich who supported him.

Excitement was so great that the Republicans gathered before the courthouse in Meadville on March 4, 1807, listened to an address by Farrelly condemning Burr and then paraded through the streets with an effigy of Burr that was ultimately burned in the public square. A wholesale riot was narrowly missed when the Federalists retaliated. They took offense at this demonstration, rightfully claiming that it was aimed at them. First, they dangled their own effigy—a caricature of Farrelly—on a signpost in front of the Republican headquarters on Water Street. Afterward, it was taken down and carried with drum and fife past the home of Farrelly, where it was "attacked and beat in a ruffian-like manner" by Pieter Huidekoper, brother of Harm Jan.

What happened after this is anyone's guess. Old scores were settled as some fighting broke out. A number of arrests followed. The medical journal of Dr. Thomas Kennedy shows that, on that day, Pieter Huidekoper had to have a number of wounds dressed. Atkinson must have delighted in Pieter's misfortune for he didn't particularly care for the Huidekopers. The high-strung Pieter, regardless of his politics, if he had any, was a noted brawler. His drinking habits and his fisticuffs eventually cost him his job with the Holland Land Company at Batavia.

Regardless of the excitement and the amount of space given in the newspapers to Burr, his enterprise and those men whose lives were affected by the chain of events, it is hard to assess the political capital the Republicans may have gained from all of this. They did attain a smashing victory in the 1808 elections, but they were unable to dislodge Federalist strength in Meadville and Mead Township. Political conservatism would remain strong in these areas long after the Federalist Party faded nationally and regionally. Many bad feelings caused by the Burr incident would heal in time, but political factionalism deepened. A permanent two-party system emerged, and one cannot help but think that the lively events of 1806–07 contributed to its development.

HARM J. HUIDEKOPER

Early Promoter of the Canal System

A great deal has been written on the Pennsylvania Canal and the French Creek Feeder Canal, but virtually nothing has been recorded on the role played by one of their promoters, Harm J. Huidekoper. Years prior to Meadville's groundbreaking ceremonies for the feeder in August 1827, this local agent for the Holland Land Company had labored diligently and effectively to have the county and northwestern Pennsylvania become a part of the state's canal system.

Huidekoper viewed the canal as indispensable to economic development. He believed in Henry Clay's American System, which encouraged economic nationalism through a national bank, tariff and internal improvements. Writing to Paul Busti in April 1824, he expressed hope that the completion of the Erie Canal in New York (it opened the next year) would provide a cash market for local surpluses. Congress was to assist by providing protection to the manufacturing and agricultural interests of western Pennsylvania. "All we want here," he wrote, "is capital and industry to render this section of Pennsylvania one of the most inviting and attractive in the Union."

What concerned him was the local depression that followed the Panic of 1819. While land values and farm prices staggered, the number of people without property increased; many were leaving the county. Both markets and money dried up. Huidekoper complained bitterly of conditions. He had taken cattle in lieu of cash from settlers indebted to him, but he lost heavily in the experiment. What was needed in the community, in his opinion, was a better grade of settlers, for the first

Harm J. Huidekoper. *Crawford County Historical Society.*

arrivals had brought nothing with them "but their hands." When the Northwestern Bank of Pennsylvania in Meadville failed in 1822, he took action against its trustees in federal court. He had about $8,000 of the land company's assets deposited in the bank.

Not only did Huidekoper have answers to the economic problems, but he was also sure he had the right answers. He believed the scarcity of money was the cause of most regional difficulties and attributed the shortage to the excessive buying of foreign goods. To counter this, he urged an austerity program, the purchase of American products only and the intense development of regional agriculture and husbandry. His economics seemed uncomplicated and conventional. Area farmers would raise more than they needed, and their surpluses would bring in desired cash. Better roads and a good canal system were necessary to market the surpluses, as well as a benevolent Congress to protect the producers.

Assuming that the federal government would cooperate by protecting local industries and financing internal improvements, Huidekoper's plan was simple enough, but his assumptions were not always valid. Poor farmers, who for more than two decades had suffered the brunt of the land system and who had stood alone in their struggle for survival, were now being singled out and asked to make sacrifices to help restore the sagging economy. Huidekoper's textbook advice to them was to raise bigger crops, breed better stock and give up tea and coffee—foreign items that "drain our country [valley] annually of enormous sums." The farmer would not be giving up anything but a bad habit!

Maybe so. Yet an examination of ledgers of two local merchants who dealt with both rich and poor indicates that only small quantities of tea and coffee were consumed. Again, among the poor and the very poor classes, little cash was used to buy anything. Barter was still a universal way of doing business. Had Huidekoper and his associates compared the outlay of cash for these beverages to what they were paying for imported brandies, wines and fabrics, they may have been embarrassed by the disparity.

Shortly after writing to Busti in early 1824, Huidekoper joined other businessmen in demanding a canal system for the state. When a number of Philadelphians asked him to assist them in planning internal improvements, he declined the offer because of personal expense involved, but he agitated on their behalf. He was sure that, because of the "imbecility" of the state government, canal enthusiasts would have to look to the federal government for necessary funding. The commonwealth bowed to public pressure, however, and its legislature began to consider proposals for an east–west canal system. Pennsylvanians feared that, in the future, commerce from the Ohio Valley could hardly be expected to go overland from Pittsburgh to Philadelphia when it would be so much easier to reach the Erie Canal. Worried citizens of Pittsburgh and Philadelphia anticipated their cities falling behind New York in both business establishments and prosperity. Huidekoper, in a letter to William

Meredith of Philadelphia, expressed confidence that, with the proposed canal, the state would progress more in five years than it would in twenty without it.

Once the legislature had authorized the governor to appoint canal commissioners to locate possible routes to Pittsburgh, Huidekoper lobbied feverishly to have an extension from that city to Lake Erie. He had little difficulty in convincing merchants of Erie and Meadville of such a need. Local men who assisted Huidekoper included Arthur Cullum, John B. Wallace, Thomas Atkinson and Judge Henry Shippen. In 1825, this group raised money to send Cullum and Wallace to a canal-planning conference in Harrisburg to represent the interests of Northwest Pennsylvania. Wallace kept Huidekoper fully informed of the proceedings. Huidekoper also relied on his good friend Henry Baldwin to help in the efforts. At the time, Baldwin was pressuring the canal commissioners to make sure the western terminus of the canal would be in Pittsburgh and not across the river in the community of Allegheny City.

The lobbying efforts of both Huidekoper and Baldwin paid off. Each got what he wanted. Having the Erie extension of the Main Line Canal approved, however, raised another question: what was the best possible route? In February 1826, the legislature approved a navigable feeder from French Creek to the summit west of Conneaut Lake. Southward from the summit there were two possible routes: one by way of the Shenango and Beaver to the Ohio, the other by way of French Creek and the Allegheny River. Each route had its enthusiastic supporters. Candidates for the General Assembly from the western counties identified with either the "western" or "eastern" route. The entire matter became politicized. It seemed that every town and community in the northwestern region of the state claimed the right to be included in the extension route. The result was constant bickering and long delays in construction.

Huidekoper contributed to the confusion. Though admitting that the western route was shorter and perhaps cheaper to construct, he still believed the commonwealth should opt for the other route because it could easily connect with other canals being contemplated as part of the state system. He requested that several members of Congress ask the engineers to survey the eastern route. Later, he was thrilled to learn that the engineers were on their way.

Captain Dickson's boat on the French Creek Feeder Canal in Meadville. *Crawford County Historical Society.*

One concern he may have had was the possibility that, should a strong enough argument be made in favor of linking the Pennsylvania Main Line with the Ohio system near New Castle, the extension from Beaver might not be funded. Ohio did approve a crosscut canal to complete the connection. Some western Pennsylvanians opposed the Erie extension, probably because they believed the Pittsburgh area would benefit more by tapping the Ohio country than by accommodating the northwest counties. Regardless, the Beaver to Erie route was finally approved.

Even this decision did not end the controversy. Though Huidekoper resigned himself to the decision, many did not. They continued to agitate for the eastern route. Their intensity matched that of Erie residents who debated the question of where the lake terminus should be—the city of Erie or the mouth of Elk Creek? Obviously, Huidekoper was unhappy with the long delays caused by the wrangling. Differences had to be resolved—and soon! He also expressed rancor toward the canal commissioners. Writing to J.J. Vanderkemp in 1827, he accused them of being apathetic toward the northwest region, where they had consented to do survey work only "to keep us happy."

Huidekoper continued to work with Erie's leaders. It was 1838, however, before ground for the canal was broken in that city. Four years later, the commonwealth refused to appropriate any more money for the project but did approve legislation incorporating the Erie Canal Company to finish the work. The first boats reached Erie in 1844.

For Huidekoper and others, the completion of the extension may have come too late. Much of the initial enthusiasm for the canal had worn off. Railroad mania was sweeping across the state. As early as 1825, Huidekoper had testified to the great advantages of rail transportation. He did not live long enough to see the first locomotive steam through Meadville, but he was remembered by those who did as a pioneer who had labored hard to revolutionize the transportation of the county and Northwest Pennsylvania.

JUSTICES OFTEN DISAPPOINT
PRESIDENTS WHO APPOINT THEM

John G. Roberts Jr. was recently appointed chief justice of the U.S. Supreme Court. Rancor over his selection was not nearly as vicious as it had been with a previous nominee, Clarence Thomas. Still, extremists judged Roberts less by his skills than by the way he was perceived to stand on the issues. This is understandable because the selection process is essentially political.

The Constitution does not specify qualification for appointment to the nation's highest court. There is no age limitation, residence requirement or stipulation that a justice be native born (six were not). In fact, candidates need not have any legal training, although all of them did. Justices come from various backgrounds. Many were former legislators, governors or diplomats.

So what does a president look for in a candidate? Party membership or support has always been important. No doubt this was a major factor in the nomination of Roberts. Yet some presidents have been willing to cross party lines, beginning with Abraham Lincoln's appointment of Stephen J. Field, a Democrat. A few have been accused of "cronyism" or, simply, "packing the court" with friends and allies. This group includes Andrew Jackson, Franklin D. Roosevelt and Lyndon Johnson.

Every president wants to select someone who will be supportive. Often there is disappointment. Sitting on the high bench has liberated some justices from earlier, possibly partisan, convictions. George Washington had problems with John Rutledge; likewise, Thomas Jefferson with William Johnson and Dwight D. Eisenhower with Earl Warren. The

Justice Henry Baldwin. *Crawford County Historical Society.*

former general allegedly remarked that his appointment of Warren was "the biggest damn-fool thing I ever did."

Another appointment that didn't turn out as initially planned was that of Henry Baldwin, who began his legal career in Meadville and eventually built his retirement home here (Baldwin-Reynolds House). After moving to Pittsburgh, he got heavily involved in politics and successfully ran for Congress in 1816. He served three terms and then resigned because of ill health. While in Congress, Baldwin became a leading protectionist, but he was unable to have his version of the tariff adopted.

Also significant was his defense of General Andrew Jackson, the hero of the Battle of New Orleans. After he had brazenly crossed the border into Spanish Florida to apprehend banditti and Native Americans who were raiding American settlements in Georgia, Jackson was vilified by members of President James Monroe's administration for embarrassing the nation. In Congress, Henry Clay declared that Jackson's actions were illegal and unconstitutional.

Baldwin disagreed. No one better supported the general. His defense was on legal grounds. Jackson's actions, Baldwin insisted, were not in violation of the Constitution for that document was never intended to protect renegades. He helped prevent serious censure and punishment of the general by Congress. Jackson never forgot this.

In 1830, Andrew Jackson named him to the court. Baldwin had been the most charismatic political figure in the commonwealth and had helped elect Jackson in the 1828 presidential election. The two men shared common ground on some issues. Both criticized federal funding for local improvements, entertained bias toward the Native Americans, upheld slavery where it existed and opposed at first the national bank.

Jackson wanted Baldwin to apply braking action to the nationalistic sway of the court. The two agreed that the judicial activism of Chief Justice John Marshall was making the court dominant over the legislative and executive branches. Baldwin tried but failed. His frustration led to antagonism, frequent dissents and violent outbursts that made some believe he was insane.

Baldwin was too independent to be a blind follower of anyone, including the president. He admitted to not being mainstream; his unpredictability was too much for both his allies and opponents. He differed with Jackson over the legitimacy of the national bank and watched the president kill that institution with a veto of the recharter bill. Jackson denounced the bank as unconstitutional, a view once shared by Baldwin before his appointment. Baldwin refused to accept Jackson's position that he, the president, was the final interpreter of the Constitution.

Baldwin was an originalist, someone who holds that courts and judges have a limited role and that the Constitution must be taken as its framers had intended. More recent originalists on the bench include Justice Antonin Scalia and former Chief Justice William Rehnquist. Baldwin defended the rights of states and those of the slave owner. While he opposed slavery, he could not deny its legality in states that allowed it because its ultimate sanction rested in the Constitution. The only way to abolish slavery was through the amendment process, which was done with the Thirteenth Amendment, some twenty years after Baldwin's death.

Jackson did not get everything he wanted from Baldwin's jurisprudence. He became very annoyed with Baldwin's preaching about the separation of powers and how the president must have greater respect for treaties. But they remained good friends. When Baldwin threatened to resign, Jackson talked him out of it. He may have later regretted not having accepted the resignation.

Will President George Bush have regrets for having nominated Robert? Who knows. He will not be in office long enough to see the impact of his nominee's jurisprudence. Years from now, when he decides to have his memoirs written, Bush may confess to having made a mistake with Roberts. But maybe not. Some presidents never want to admit to error.

DIRECT PRIMARY HAS
COUNTY ROOTS

Many voters, including politicians, do not like the primary system in its present form. Among their objections are the costs involved, the absence of a national primary day and the seemingly endless prattle of the candidates.

I understand the pain of these voters. However, not wishing to open debate on the pros and cons of a uniquely American process that has been evolving for nearly two centuries, I thought I would instead look to the beginnings of the direct primary here in our county.

Meeting in 1842, the Democrats of Crawford County expressed dissatisfaction with their nominating convention as a method of choosing candidates. They had hoped that, by replacing the old caucus system, a convention of township delegates selecting candidates would bring the electoral process closer to the people. The caucus had given party bosses too much discretionary power in naming nominees. Unfortunately, the same people who had controlled the caucus often ended up manipulating the convention.

After convening and failing to agree on a slate, the township delegates called for a general meeting of the party faithful to address the crisis. Time was running out before the general election. In early August, a surprising number of Democrats from nearly every township packed the Presbyterian church near the courthouse in Meadville. At this meeting, George Shellito of Sadsbury introduced resolutions proposing a fundamental change in the way candidates were to be chosen. His bold move led to squabbling and confusion that nearly sent the delegates running to the doors. Cooler

Official Returns of the Election held in Crawford County, OCTOBER, 1843.

DISTRICTS.	Samuel Hays.	James Darghy.	James Clarke.	Jesse Miller.	W. B. Foster.	William Theod.	Benjamin Weaver.	Simeon Guilford.	Alexander Power.	Wm. P. Shattuck.	James R. Kerr.	Daniel Dence.	Samuel Forker.	Finlaw Beatty.	John E. Smith.	Joseph Cochran.
	CONGRESS.		CANAL COMMISSIONERS.						ASSEMBLY			CO. COMMISS. TREAS. AUDIT.				
Borough,	153	68	134	134	134	104	102	103	49	214	161	28	178	70	172	149
Mead Township,	113	89	102	102	102	52	52	52	71	134	69	26	120	37	136	107
Vernon,	100	30	103	103	104	31	31	31	101	52	51	11	76	67	115	96
Woodcock,	157	16	136	138	138	62	62	62	108	134	113	17	132	75	160	118
Rockdale,	19	17	22	22	22	14	14	14	16	26	23	10	18	19	27	23
Richmond,	33	12	18	18	18	17	17	17	22	40	44		14	40	22	20
Athens,	33	4	17	17	17	13	13	13	16	18	38	1	17	21	29	30
Rome,	76	1	59	59	59	14	14	14	15	25	100	2	51	42	73	63
Sparta,	30		28	28	25				13	18	60		25	17	26	19
Bloomfield,	12	24	9	9	9	17	17	17	6	30	32	2	25	11	32	26
Oil Creek,	95	17	68	68	68	25	25	25	3	18	130	33	60	47	81	46
Randolph,	54	3	46	46	46	17	17	17	42	40	46	6	28	46	64	63
Troy,	27		26	26	25				12	5	31	3	15	13	23	22
Wayne,	36		36	36	36	1	1	1	28	29	13		7	23	40	41
Fairfield,	154	2	136	133	133	29	29	29	133	102	51	22	41	135	150	146
Greenwood,	143		144	141	141				154	17	2	5	93	43	143	131
Sadsbury,	71	2	69	70	70	29	29	29	36	76	67	3	37	54	77	36
East Fallowfield,	67		68	68	68				67	41	2	3	67		68	65
West Fallowfield,	49	9	50	59	50	10	10	10	14	55	15	1	51	7	63	48
South Shenango,	107		90	99	99	13	13	13	76	106	11	7	96	17	108	111
North Shenango,	61	24	63	63	63	7	7	7	66	58	34	5	61	22	84	54
Beaver,	36	29	36	36	36	30	30	30	59		64	7	37	27	39	37
Conneaut,	22	21	20	20	20	32	32	32	53	12	65		11	44	7	9
Spring,	87	11	91	91	91	90	90	90	95	49	95	8	85	90	86	85
Summit,	73	47	91	91	91	31	31	31	91	89	60	13	60	70	102	75
Sommerhill,	77	3	71	71	71	23	23	23	93	11	78	2	47	47	69	69
Hayfield,	63	14	72	72	72	83	83	83	87	80	53	21	76	44	107	61
Cussewago,	38	10	34	34	34	16	16	16	48	31	21	1	31	25		31
Venango,	91	13	110	110	110	22	22	22	31	122	78		109	22	73	44
Total,	2107	402	1951	1954	1951	757	758	756	1605	1621	1629	237	1668	1158	2214	1644

Election returns—county results at the time of the direct primary. *Crawford County Historical Society.*

Rooster v. raccoon. Representative symbols of the Democrat Party (rooster) and the Whig Party (raccoon). *Crawford County Historical Society.*

heads managed to refocus the group's attention to the problem before them, and the Shellito reforms were unanimously adopted.

Since time was a factor, Shellito proposed that, on September 9, Democrats meet in their respective townships, select officers and ballot for one candidate for each office to be filled. Eligible persons seeking office had to announce their intentions three weeks prior to the township meeting.

After the balloting, township chairmen were to assemble at the courthouse on September 13 and tabulate their returns. The persons receiving the highest number of votes would be declared nominated for the General Assembly and local offices.

What occurred here was somewhat reminiscent of what had happened a generation earlier to the county's Democratic Republicans (not to be confused with later Republicans). When a number of them decided to nominate David Mead for Congress in 1810, they had to do it in an unprecedented fashion.

A sudden call for a district conference to pick a candidate for Congress had caught local Republicans unprepared. They had no time to select township delegates. The congressional district consisted of Allegheny and the counties to the north, so communication was a problem. Quickly assembling in Meadville as many county Republicans as possible on such short notice, the party nominated Mead and appointed delegates to the district conference with instructions to press for Mead's candidacy.

As it turned out, Mead dropped out of the race because of intraparty bickering. Thomas Atkinson, of the *Crawford Weekly Messenger*, called Mead's factions "worthless and unprincipled." The county delegates then switched to Abner Lacock of Beaver, who went on to defeat Adamson Tannehill of Allegheny.

The "Crawford County System" spread to other counties and some of the states. But not until the twentieth century, when the Progressive movement divided both major parties, did the direct primary come into general use. In 1903, Wisconsin adopted a mandatory statewide primary law. Today, the primary is used in some form throughout the nation.

Often, the most annoying pain is the pain of time. Waiting for something to happen can seem eternal. We view the direct primary, for example, as something good for voter participation in the electoral process. Still, after every tedious campaign, many of us cannot help but wait for changes in the system.

Presidential candidate John Kerry once commented, "America shouldn't have to put up with eight months of sniping." That is a point well taken. And he was just referring to the time he would be jawboning with President George Bush. He could have also added the several months he had wrestled with Democratic rivals.

We constantly fret about the way we run our primaries and campaigns. Still, except for a few states changing their primary dates, we return to basically the same long, drawn-out process every election year. This is politics. Maybe we just have to admit that we like it this way.

NOTHING REMAINS OF CRAWFORD COUNTY'S EARLIEST COMMUNE

A newcomer to town recently asked me what I remembered about the "Hippie Farm" of Oz near Harmonsburg during the 1960s. After I had given him what little information I had, he wanted to know if this social experiment was without precedent.

I didn't wish to debate whether Oz had been an experiment of any kind; instead, I turned my friend's attention to earlier efforts of communal life in the county. Prior to the Civil War, the most memorable had to be the New Richmond Phalanx near Hickory Corners.

Nearly everything we know about this commune comes to us through the *Crawford Democrat* and oral tradition. Many years ago, Mary Chapin Warner White collected for her *Annals of Lyons Hollow* stories from descendants of those who were either members of the phalanx or were in a position to know something about it. Maybe as many as one hundred men, women and children belonged. Names included Daniel Hunt, Abel Cross, Samuel Little, David Stewart and Enos Corey. Some in the community, including Daniel Hunt's brother Ebenezer, did not approve of communalism and therefore refused to join.

In January 1845, the *Crawford Democrat* published articles of association that had been adopted by the group. Among the purposes was the promotion of agriculture, manufacturing, the arts and sciences and education. Religious and political opinions were not to be a bar to admission or grounds for expulsion. Intoxicants could not be made or sold.

Only resident males of legal age could vote. Everyone chose his line of work. All residents paid rent and were entitled to a free education.

Phalanx Building. *Painting in the possession of the Crawford County Historical Society.*

Orphans, the sick and those unable to take care of themselves were provided for. The family remained integral in the new community, and proper behavior was expected at all times.

Evidently, a number of cabins and houses were built to accommodate the members. One was a large L-shaped frame structure, some one hundred by fifty feet, with a huge kitchen and dining room, brass doorknobs and carpeting. Many years ago, the late Joe Davis of Hemlock Hollows took me to the site where the buildings once stood.

The Richmond group followed the utopian socialism as outlined by the French philosopher Charles Fourier. Through a system of *phalanges* (phalanxes), Fourier hoped for an ideal society based on harmony. He demanded that capital and labor work together to end the degrading condition of workers caused by the Industrial Revolution and the weaknesses of a competitive economy. To him, self-sufficient communal units, or associations, were the answer. He thought of each unit as a joint-stock company in which residents invested their money, worked together

Ebenezer Hunt, brother of Daniel Hunt. He did not join Phalanx. *Crawford County Historical Society.*

and profited through their labors. The Richmond group boasted of having already $10,000 in subscription, a tidy amount for the day. Shares sold for $50 each.

Fourierism found many disciples, including prominent editor Horace Greeley. From New England to Wisconsin, a network of phalanxes represented the hopes of disillusioned Americans. Most of the country still faced hard times following the Panic of 1837. Banks were in trouble, the national debt was soaring and land values were down. In addition to all of this, slavery and the Texas question politically divided the country.

Some of these phalanxes were temporarily successful, but most failed within a few months. The idea of selfless cooperation seemed to run counter to the rugged individualism that spirited American expansion of the nineteenth century. The New Richmond group also floundered. Greed, misunderstanding and laziness had apparently contributed to the demise. As living conditions worsened, bitterness set in, and members bickered with one another. By the early 1850s, we suspect that the noble venture was over.

Still, the phalanx was not without good times. Outsiders who were invited to break bread often spoke of the warm hospitality. The wedding of Pamelia Corey in 1845 was a gala affair. A sumptuous dinner followed a beautiful ceremony. The publisher of the *Crawford Democrat* was there, enjoyed himself and later wrote, "We like to see such kinds of association, and have no doubt most of our young friends of both sexes will agree with us that they should become more frequent."

Public endorsement by a newspaper not known for its liberalism may seem strange. Yet communalism was no stranger than two other movements considered radical at the time: abolitionism and spiritualism. Each of these, in some way, responded to the cries of a difficult age.

We may never learn the full story of the New Richmond Phalanx, but we can assume that the members were sincere in the hope of bettering their lives. And for this, we should remember them.

YES . . . SPARE THE ROD

Early Educator Rejected Corporal Punishment

The *Meadville Tribune* reporter Mary Spicer's recent provocative article "Should schools spare the rod?" re-sparked debate on a question that has tormented educators ever since Pennsylvania's "free school" law of 1834. Education has changed, but the issue persists.

A Pennsylvanian who examined corporal punishment 150 years ago was Samuel P. Bates of Meadville. Best remembered as a historian who wrote highly acclaimed books on the Civil War, Bates was also a nationally noted educator. Born in Massachusetts, he came to Meadville to teach ancient languages at the academy after graduating in 1851 from Brown University. He soon became the school's principal. It was a time when public education was becoming more popular. Later, he went from being county superintendent to general deputy superintendent of schools in the commonwealth.

In this latter capacity, he inspected county schools, their curricula and staffs. Generally, he found deplorable conditions. Facilities were inadequate, teachers were poorly trained and paid and school boards were generally opposed to raising taxes to attack the deficiencies.

It was tough being a Harrisburg watchdog. Improving the schools was simply not easy. Many citizens resented the state meddling in local affairs like education. Reluctant school officials opposed the '34 law and eventually helped defeat from reelection Governor George Wolfe, a strong supporter of that law. They were mired in a realism that focused upon control, costs and the question of whether every child could benefit from free schooling. Bates argued for an assertive amalgam of the

Samuel P. Bates. *Crawford County Historical Society.*

Central School, North Shenango, one of the first schools in the commonwealth to become a part of the consolidated school movement. *Crawford County Historical Society.*

practical with the visionary, a progressive maxim that would underpin any educational order.

Everywhere Bates went, his message was clear: education had to be liberal, open to every child and publicly financed. He was a progressive ahead of his time. In addition to hiring qualified teachers, he urged that school districts provide physical education, better texts and programs for the handicapped. He also encouraged both institutes and normal schools (colleges) to prepare teachers. He had his recommended reforms published in the *Pennsylvania School Journal* and the *American Journal of Education*, and eventually they were adopted.

Bates foresaw classroom discipline as a troubling clog in the learning process. Corporal punishment was repugnant to him. He realized that he represented a minority view, but he failed to see how paddling, or even threatening, a child physically made the child a more responsive student.

Throughout the commonwealth, he watched teachers apply the rod freely, often too freely. Spanking a child before the class created disorder in the one-room school and terrified the other children. He also noted that teachers had, regrettably, often been hired simply to enforce order. Their ability to handle bullies often compensated for their inability to spell or do fractions better than some of their students.

"Knowledge gained by compulsion and under the influence of fear," Bates wrote, "is of little worth and is not apt long to be remembered." To make discipline more important than the pursuit of knowledge implies that the child cannot learn anything in an easy, enjoyable manner. Instead, the student worries what may happen if the pen is held wrong, a word mispronounced or a line of poetry forgotten. As a consequence, children under such constant pressure "study with tears in their eyes." Learning thus becomes dreadful, meaningless, a painful must. Little wonder why so many young people want to leave school as soon as they can.

Bates feared corporal punishment as a threat to public education and, in turn, to the democratic process. Countries with unstable or nondemocratic governments, he believed, are those with uneducated citizens. And he faulted those governments where monarchs and churches control education. The quote "Education unrestricted is the first element of national liberty" best summarized his feelings. Following this conviction with an equally strong dictum, he wrote, "The man who can neither read nor write is not a fit person to exercise the elective franchise."

Like most progressive thinkers of the mid-nineteenth century, Bates pondered the future of education. "We have looked at education [too] objectively," he exclaimed. The personal relationship between the teacher and pupil, so important, was rapidly disappearing. Teachers have been degraded to a menial position by "dull and lifeless" textbooks that have taken over the classroom. He regretted that teaching had never been treated either as a science or a learned profession.

The progress achieved to date in public education, I am sure, pleases most of us, but would Bates be impressed were he alive today? In many ways, the answer is yes. Since he spun his educational philosophy, however, only two dozen or so states have banned corporal punishment. In Pennsylvania, most school districts have done likewise. So, despite more than a century of advances in education, psychology, medicine, etc., we still remain divided as a nation on this question of human behavior.

To be sure, Bates would be up front today supporting global initiatives to end all corporal punishment. Meanwhile, he might cynically ask his fellow Crawford Countians, "Still paddling the students?" How unconscionable.

FIRST LOCAL REPUBLICANS JOINED
TOGETHER TO ELECT LINCOLN

S. Newton Pettis must have had a tear in his eyes as he stood in the chilly November air and welcomed the festive crowd outside his home. "Hurrah for President Lincoln!" someone shouted. "Hurrah for the Union!" In the background, cannons boomed and victory fires blazed. Through the flickering light of dozens of torches, the future judge could make out the familiar faces of many friends who made up the Lincoln Guards, the Meadville Wide-Awakes and other Republican groups. The long ordeal was over. Lincoln's party had won.

A year earlier, the editor of the *Crawford Journal* had predicted that the election of 1860 would be a "contest that will…live in history long after those who shall participate in the strife shall have passed away."

Pettis and his friends would have agreed. No previous campaign had been fought with such ominous implications as the one just prior to the Civil War. Slavery tainted all of the issues of the campaign, and understandably so. Viewed emotionally, Lincoln's victory was a victory for Union and Freedom. From the standpoint of Crawford County politics, it was also a smashing triumph for a party that, only several years earlier, local Democratic boss James E. McFarland had predicted would enjoy a very short life.

McFarland alluded to Lincoln's party being a conglomeration of political hybrids—former Whigs, Freesoilers, Abolitionists, Know-Nothings, temperance advocates and Liberty Party members—men whose diverse political philosophies could not keep them together for long. Many Republicans had to agree. Before their first taste of victory in 1856, a number of them had refused to support their own local candidates. Why? Because some of the candidates who had previously denounced freesoilism (nonextension of slavery) were now supporting it, for it was the heart of the Republican platform.

Others just seemed hopelessly confused. The editor of the *Conneautville Courier*, A.J. Mason, was one Republican cynic who "smelled a rat" and withdrew his support. Like other purists, he lamented the fact that the new party had become a haven for unprincipled opportunists so mired in their own hypocrisies that they could not help but babble absurdities. For example, how could former Know-Nothings, those apostles of nativism who had attacked Irish and German immigrants—especially if they were Catholic—now turn around and scream for freedom and equality for all men regardless of color?

Obviously, McFarland was wrong in his prediction. The new party did indeed have a future, although it was attracting mavericks. He was wrong not because he had failed to understand the true character of his opponents, but because he had misread the political vibrations of the day. Strange times produce strange moods, and the decade of the 1850s was far from normal. Often, periods of national stress produce ideals and martyrdom that rise above the ambitions and avarice of office-seekers and party hacks. To some degree, this was true of the decade preceding the Civil War. For one thing, the astute politician could see that slavery had suddenly become immune to further compromise. Either you were for it or against it. Thus, it was causing a mirage of the entire political surface. Whether this was a temporary condition made little difference. The important thing was that slavery, for the moment, had become the liveliest issue since the revolutionary movement of the eighteenth century. Used properly, it could lead a party to quick victory.

This is how the Republicans saw it. Once slavery had established itself as the primary issue, it was only a matter of time before expediency dictated a truce among the hybrids. The success of the party would depend upon how well its members responded to that issue. Besides, where could the old Whigs and Know-Nothings go? Their national parties had been destroyed by the very forces that were now driving the stake into the heart of the Democratic Party. Whigs like Alfred Huidekoper, John Dick and Hiram L. Richmond had little choice. Why try to mend a political Humpty-Dumpty, which their local party had become, when the parent

Alfred Huidekoper, son of Harm J. Huidekoper. *Crawford County Historical Society.*

organization was dead? It would be much easier to fashion the new Republican Party to their liking to serve their own interests.

But slavery was a gut issue and defied routine assimilation. When combined with the idea of equality—which both gradual and immediate abolition implied—it challenged the Northern conscience. While Erie Republicans called for its abolition, Crawford Republicans, following the national platform, asked only that slavery be excluded from the territories. This was the moderate course that most of them preferred. Some feared that the expansion of slavery would lead to "amalgamation" (miscegenation), something that had to be avoided. Blacks must be separated entirely from the white man and perhaps colonized. This could be done with good Republicanism! By this time, no Northerner wanted to be associated with the abominable institution, but few spoke in favor of racial equality or civil rights.

When Freesoilers S. Newton Pettis and John Howe said they didn't wish to see slavery extend beyond its present boundaries, they meant it, but then so did most county Democrats. Unfortunately for the latter, they just happened to be on the wrong side of the issue. After all, it was their party the slaveholding oligarchy in the South belonged to. Nevertheless, they damned the "black Republican Fusion Party"—the "Freedom Shriekers"—for exploiting the slavery question at the risk of destroying the Union.

Most of the county Republicans were former Whigs. Those who were businessmen, and many were, reacted less to the agitation over slavery than to the bread-and-butter issues the national Republicans were adding to their growing platform. Internal improvements, high tariffs, sound money and banking and the development of the West with free homesteads—these were the real issues that would win votes among a responsible electorate in the North. But none of these could be achieved without first accepting the antislavery plank.

After the 1856 election, unity of purpose—total defeat of the Democratic Party—became the single objective of the local Republicans. Personal whim and mobility were to give way to party solidarity. But keeping the ranks closed was not always that easy. When the venerable John Dick, contrary to the wish of the party, decided to run an "independent candidacy" for Congress in 1858, he was severely chastised by the Republican press. Such freewheeling tactics were not allowed. Dick was definitely out of bounds.

Admittedly, the Republicans didn't have the organization and discipline enjoyed by their opponents. But they overcame these deficiencies by developing committees of vigilance and rally groups to drum up enthusiasm, keep an eye on the Democrats and get out the vote. Committeemen included S.A. Torbett of Meadville, J.W. Patten of Conneautville, Henry Saeger of Saegertown and H.L. Logan of Venango. Their efforts paid off. Part of the strategy was to flood the district with a team of speakers, notable among whom were H.L. Richmond, H.H. Henderson, John Howe and S. Newton Pettis. National Republicans were also invited to help support local candidates. A good friend of the Freesoilers, J.R. Giddings of Ohio, spoke at the courthouse in June 1860. Simon Cameron, Ben Wade and David Wilmot were other big party names who shuttled between Meadville and Erie. Until Lincoln received the nomination, Cameron had been the top choice for the presidency among the local Republicans. Old-line Whigs and even some Democrats would endorse him because of his stand for good protective tariff.

On the eve of the presidential election of 1860, county Republicans stood on solid ground. If differences still existed among them, they quickly vanished before the specter of four more years of government dominated by "slavocrats." Actually, the Democrats appeared licked. Their national convention in Charleston had ended in shambles, with the delegates pulling apart along sectional and ideological lines. This was comforting to the Republicans who, nevertheless, shrugged off all tendencies toward complacency. Instead, they picked up the campaign pace with more demonstrations, marches and free-swinging programs that kept the voters alert. Pettis and Howe were making speeches everywhere. The Meadville Wide-Awakes visited various communities, drumming up enthusiasm that swelled Republican pride and intensified Democratic apathy. Nothing but defeatism faced the oldest party in the county.

The county Republicans gave Andrew Curtin, the party's choice for governor, over two thousand votes from more than eight thousand ballots. Curtin and Pettis were good friends; the two had worked together to secure Lincoln's nomination in Chicago the previous spring. The culmination of all Republican efforts, however, came in November, when Lincoln's margin of victory was even greater than Curtin's.

The campaign had been a hard one, and now congratulations were in order. When cheering Republicans gathered in front of the Pettis home that November evening, they were expressing their gratitude to a man who had towered above other men in the recent battle. Graciously, he reciprocated by thanking them for their tireless efforts to keep the party together, the issue alive and the public interest afire. They understood what they had succeeded in doing. Pennsylvania had been considered the key state in the election, and they had managed to deliver it to Lincoln. Their party and leader now held the power to decide the fate of the republic.

Smoke settled in thick layers over the city of Meadville that night—smoke from torches, cannons, victory fires and fireworks. Several months later, another kind of smoke would hover over a battle area far to the south—Fort Sumter. One signified the glory of victory; the other, death and disunion. How many of the merrymakers foretold the holocaust that would soon follow? Not many, probably. Most likely, the majority sized up the political situation as did the editor of the *Crawford Journal* on November 6, 1860, when he wrote: "Abraham Lincoln will be elected, and there will be no disunion or bloodshed."

A SOLDIER WRITES OF HIS CIVIL WAR EXPERIENCE

No event in American history has been chronicled as often as the Civil War. Military books continue to line shelves in libraries and bookstores. A reason for this phenomenon is the constant uncovering of diaries and memoirs of Union and Confederate soldiers. Before they were donated to libraries, universities and historical societies, many of these accounts were held by descendants who, understandably, were in no hurry to relinquish them.

The diary of George Spitler is a good example. Recently donated to the Crawford County Historical Society by his grandson, Don Leberman of Meadville, it gives a vivid picture of army life during the Civil War by a combat soldier who volunteered shortly after General Robert E. Lee's invasion of Pennsylvania in the summer of 1863. Serving his country, he believed, was the right thing to do.

Every war diary is rich in emotions, images and perceptions. Spitler's is no exception. He saw the war as being necessary, but it was still a nightmare to every soldier who expected, at any moment, to be a combat casualty or moribund from dysentery or malaria. He wrote of the tedium, loneliness, endless hours of drilling or doing picket duty and of finally going into combat. Living in a tent was not like home; army chow was not like his wife's cooking. But Spitler did not complain—at least not openly.

Two themes run throughout the diary: Spitler's patriotism and his religious faith. He was willing to do his share of the fighting, but it was his faith and letters from home that sustained him every day. The constant stress was evident; he suffered from frequent headaches. He attended prayer meetings, where he often preached. The heavy drinking, gambling and profanity that dominated camp life offended him. He wrote of "the wickedness with which we are surrounded." Even the behavior of some officers with their "ladies" was disgraceful.

"It is a shame that we are compelled to serve under such men," he wrote. "They punish enlisted men for vices they themselves commit." He blamed the war for causing men to act this way. It was as if they had lost what faith they still possessed and had given up.

Army life was tough for a man even when he was not being shot at. Officers meted out corporal punishment, which could be severe. Desertion and sleeping on the picket line were capital offenses punishable by death. Spitler described how his captain tied a man by his thumbs to a tree for throwing stones at a freedman. On another occasion, a soldier and his "wench" were stuffed into a barrel for having committed adultery. How long the lovers remained there, Spitler didn't say.

The diet was another problem. It was less than filling, and the men complained. Spitler was not one of them, but a bit of sarcasm showed when he bragged about "all the delicacies of life which Uncle Sam sees fit to give us"—bread and coffee for breakfast, hardtack and coffee for supper!

When they departed by boat for Hilton Head, South Carolina, recruits and substitutes from the Philadelphia–New York area joined them. These were "principally bad men given to strong drinking," Spitler commented. They fought and stole from one another. One even tried to desert by jumping overboard, carrying a half dozen canteens, but he was caught. The rowdiness and storms made Spitler's maiden trip on a steamer a bad one.

On the Carolina coast, Spitler's company ("K" of the Seventy-sixth Regiment) was constantly on alert because of Rebel forces in the area. Picket duty and drills became more regular and intense. Whenever he could, he read and wrote letters. At the back of the diary, he kept a record of letters received and written.

Often, a diarist fails to see the strangeness of the situation as he describes particular events that are not logically linked. On one occasion, Spitler observed some men getting drunk, others washing their clothes and still others playing ball (probably baseball). At the dock, civilian

Musicians in the Civil War. *Crawford County Historical Society.*

An ambulance at the Battle of Antietam. *Crawford County Historical Society.*

workers loading coal dropped their shovels and refused to work until they were given their coffee! And in the background came the endless sound of shooting and exploding shells. The scene was surreal.

But, then, war is irrational. Spitler did not try to explain the politics behind all the carnage he was witnessing, other than as a rebellion of Southern states. He was a Unionist—a Republican—who was fighting to preserve the Union and freedom, yet he was not allowed to vote in the recent election. Nor did he try to fathom why, at twenty-three, married and a former teacher, he was in the South, flanked by Christians like himself and confronted by other Christians, all of whom were trying to kill one another.

On May 16, 1864, Spitler was shot through the groin at Drewry's Bluff, Virginia. A wound like this did not promise much hope for recovery. Thus, he was left on the field while others, who were not as badly wounded, were treated. Two unknown soldiers finally carried him for ten miles on a stretcher before his wound was dressed. They saved his life.

He wrote about his near-fatal experience that very same day. As expected, his handwriting was shaky compared to his usual fine penmanship. He was taken aboard a steamer and then to Fort Monroe. He suffered permanent disability.

Spitler stopped making entries shortly after being wounded and did not resume until January 1, 1865, at which time he was back home. He went for medical treatment in Philadelphia, where he learned of Lee's surrender and the assassination of Lincoln. In May, he was discharged upon his request, even though he was far from being healed. He returned home and was treated by a local physician.

After the war, he clerked at Pithole in the oil region until he moved with his family to Cussewago Township in 1868. He farmed and served as a school director. He died in 1912 and was buried in Saegertown Cemetery.

THE OIL BOOM PLEASED MANY,
BUT NOT ALL

The gold strikes of California and Alaska, and the Dakota land boom of the 1860s and '70s, sensationalized economic episodes in our past. They held thousands of "boom or bust" stories that told of fame, fortune and tragedy. A strong contender for being the greatest mania creator in American history was the oil boom of the mid-nineteenth century in our own area. It came slowly, but when it came, it shook the Western world. Even then, it did not excite everyone locally.

In 1858, the Seneca Oil Company at New Haven sent Edwin Drake to Titusville to drill for oil. They gave him the title of "colonel" to impress the residents of this little town in Crawford County. Meadville's papers gave Drake the ho-hum treatment. Editors wrote about current events that seemed more interesting to their readers, like the Republican Party's chances in the forthcoming elections and the possibility that their county may finally get a railroad. Besides, who was this Drake, they asked, and what was the big deal about oil?

The initial indifference of the editors was understood. Oil, or Seneca oil as it was commonly called in pioneer days, was familiar to the earliest settlers before Colonel Drake was born. It had been used by Native Americans for so long that not even the oldest living chief remembered if any of his ancestors could recall not using it.

The term "petroleum" can be found on a map of Pennsylvania drawn in the 1750s by Lewis Evans. Perhaps the earliest value of the slimy liquid appears in a 1797 daybook kept by William Wilson, a merchant at Fort Franklin, a little south of Meadville. Three kegs of petroleum

A gusher in the Oil Region. *Crawford County Historical Society.*

were assessed by Wilson at fifty dollars per keg. It may have come from Nathaniel Carey, who collected it from springs and peddled it as a cure for body ills.

Prior to Drake's arrival at Titusville, the Pittsburgh area already had an oil industry. By 1850, Samuel Kier started to refine petroleum derived from salt wells. His still operated just outside of the city. He promoted his product both as an illuminant and as a medical remedy for every ailment known to man—diarrhea, cholera, piles, burns, pimples, deafness, ringworm, etc. Pittsburgh itself became a center of refining "coal oil"—oil extracted from coal.

So what could this man Drake and his company do, the cynics asked, that had not been done with oil over the last century? Were they to provide more oil to the carnival charlatan to practice his quackery on innocent victims? After analyzing the black substance, American and European scientists could answer with assurance that a great deal more could be derived from this ancient and mysterious substance.

This assured optimism of top scientists, combined with the fact that Drake was receiving as much as forty dollars per barrel, was all many

Oil being transported. *Crawford County Historical Society.*

wanted to hear. Half crazed with the desire to make lots of money, county residents started to drill on their farms, in their backyards and along French Creek. Even in Meadville, the enthusiasm led to a number of digs. But there was little, if any, oil oozing in these parts.

It didn't take long for general pandemonium to set in. Plenty of outside capital and settlers poured into the region. Established residents either became a part of the madness or resisted it. Though Meadville caught the oil fever by early '61, some of its citizens found the wagons hauling the oil through their city to the trains in Linesville dangerous, disturbing and dirty. Others found being constantly pestered to sell or lease their farms to oil companies and speculators increasingly annoying.

There were other features of this craziness that were disturbing. By our standards today, the oil industry was far from being environment friendly. Photographs taken at the time tell the story. Refineries, which were sprouting as fast as the derricks, dumped their toxic waste into Oil

Oil derricks near Titusville. *Crawford County Historical Society.*

Creek. Hillsides were stripped of their trees, and harmful disposables and litter were everywhere. Equally disturbing was the general behavior of those arrivals who hoped to make a quick fortune, enjoy the best time of their lives and then leave. Drunkenness and licentiousness seemed normal for many of them, especially those who found saloons and bawdy houses more exciting than anything back home.

The economic upside easily outscored the indecent behavior of a few and the mismanagement of corporate housekeeping, at least in the minds of those who were blinded by the huge profits they were making. The 1865 oil atlas clearly shows how wild oil speculation became. By this year, oil had become one of the nation's chief exports to Europe. Obviously, local manufacturing firms and businesses benefited from all this new economy. The Civil War and the railroad were additional boosts.

Refineries, tool factories and barrel making in Meadville and Titusville were just a few of the more popular industries. In Titusville, refineries became the leading industry, with Parker, Abbott and Barnsdall being among the first established to produce illuminating oil. The city's young Theodore Barnsdall, who drilled his first well at the age of sixteen, went on to have a fabulous career in oil.

William Reynolds of Meadville, a prime mover of the Atlantic and Great Western Railroad, represented that group of early builders that believed the rails should go where the action is. He initially ran into trouble when he tried to run his railroad into the oil region. Some opponents, who viewed the oil market as purely speculative, believed a railroad's fortune must lie in what is above the ground and not what is below it. Reynolds regretted that this kind of thinking had allowed Pennsylvania Railroad and the New York Central to seize control of the oil market in the region.

The oil boom, like other economic explosions in our history, struck like lightning, peaked and then died out sooner than many had expected. The opening of the oil fields in Western states was a principal reason for the demise. Fortunately, many industries spawned by the petroleum fever, including some of the refineries, survived and even grew. The critics who had lampooned imposing Easterners with their deep pockets and greedy eyes could later quip, "I told you it would pass." Well, pass it did, but the oil boom and the industry that subsequently erupted left an indelible mark on Crawford County, especially on its manufacturing heritage.

HE WANTED TO BUILD
A RAILROAD, AND HE DID

Progress is generally the result of a group's collective action. Often, an individual from the group stands out as the driving force or catalyst behind the action. This is the case with the railroad's arrival to Crawford County and northwestern Pennsylvania. William Reynolds is remembered as the one person who refused to abandon his dream of bringing the rails to this part of Pennsylvania.

Reynolds grew up in Meadville in the first half of the nineteenth century, a period of Western expansion and the first stage of the Industrial Revolution in America. Transportation was on every businessman's agenda. A growing nation demanded its improvement with government support. Reynolds watched how his family and friends moved about in stagecoaches and, on rivers, in keelboats, steam and canalboats. By the time he attended Allegheny College, each of these modes of travel had an impact on his hometown and each had its limitations.

The locomotive fascinated him the most. Its power and energy symbolized the very strength of the young republic. Early engines, with their trailing coaches, may not have been too impressive, but they held much promise. While riding the "rails" from Harrisburg to Lancaster in 1841, Reynolds heard rumors of the rails coming to the western region of the state. He couldn't wait for it to happen.

By this time, many former developers of turnpikes and canals agitated for the railroad to come to their town. In Crawford County, with the economic situation changing, the time certainly seemed right. The canal had suddenly lost its appeal, the annoying land issue was less annoying,

William Reynolds. *Crawford County Historical Society.*

new businesses were starting and agriculture was becoming diversified. With respect to transportation, turnpikes, canals and riverboats of all kinds were no longer sufficient.

By the early 1850s, Reynolds tied the nation's future to rail transportation. He saw how local producers faced the onerous task of reaching out to intersect with expanding markets of other communities and Eastern cities. In his mind, a network of railroads had to be the solution to the problem.

Though he was a person of vision, neither he nor others could foresee the oil boom that began in 1859 or the Civil War two years later. The pressure that these two events created for the transportation systems found Crawford County unprepared to handle the extra traffic. It was not until November 1862 that the first train rolled through Meadville. After that, the county moved quickly. For the next eight years, it led all other counties in the commonwealth in laying track.

In 1851, Reynolds and a group of business leaders met to consider a plan to build a rail connection between southwestern New York and northeastern Ohio. A number of lines had already been laid or projected in those areas. Cities in Pennsylvania—Erie, Philadelphia and Pittsburgh—opposed any such connection, however, for it would primarily benefit the neighboring states. Reynolds challenged the opposition and found supporters for a branch of the Pittsburgh and Erie Railroad. The branch was later called the Meadville Railway Company.

To build the branch required a huge amount of capital. Reynolds appealed to the county commissioners who did not oppose the idea of issuing bonds but insisted that public approval be first acquired. In the summer of 1853, a campaign to enlist citizen support resulted in a decision that overwhelmingly favored the bond issue. The vote in favor of a $200,000 subscription was 3,235; against was 173. This was more than adequate to ensure the subscription and to have a groundbreaking ceremony in August.

Enlisting subscribers was not a sure thing, however. A money crunch resulted when the general economy softened. Bonds could not be sold, workers could not be hired and company general expenses could not be paid. Ready cash to meet current emergencies was advanced by Reynolds, Judge Gaylord Church and John Dick.

When both the economy and the company's financial situation continued to worsen, Pennsylvania's Supreme Court allowed the county to repudiate its bonds. The future of the railroad appeared dim. Reynolds certainly didn't intend to give up. He found a good friend in Marvin Kent of the struggling Atlantic and Great Western Railroad of Ohio. The two men concluded that local venture capital was inadequate and decided therefore to try their luck with European investors.

The Meadville Railroad, now known as the Atlantic and Great Western (A&GW) Railroad of Pennsylvania, made its stock and bonds available in England for cash and iron. James McHenry of London and Jose de Salamanca of Spain became the principal fundraisers. McHenry sent to America an engineer of some reputation, Thomas Kennard, to promote the interests of the company, submit reports and superintend the construction of the railroad. His engineering skills were effective, but his lavish lifestyle and freewheeling opinions annoyed Reynolds. His opposition to running a spur, or branch, into the oil region, for example, proved to be a strategic disaster. Reynolds blamed the shortsightedness of Kennard and McHenry for allowing the Pennsylvania Railroad and the New York Central Railroad to gain a controlling interest in this area.

Differences between Reynolds and his English partners did not go away, nor did they prevent the railroad from being built. McHenry continually complained that he was not being furnished with sufficient securities; something Reynolds found puzzling because the securities sent easily exceeded the cost of the work performed to date. Reynolds charged London with serious money mismanagement and failure to submit regular financial statements. Without them, routine audits were impossible. He also accused McHenry's agents of illegal disbursements of proceeds from bond sales. The money question haunted McHenry. At one point, he wondered what had happened to $4 million that he had remitted on Kennard's drafts! Reynolds had made his case.

Reynolds insisted on tighter control and fiscal responsibility at the same time that McHenry and Kennard sought wider authority. Since each railroad division—A&GW of Ohio, A&GW of Pennsylvania, A&GW of New York—operated independently of the other two, it was relatively easy for European investors to influence management in one of the divisions. With very huge amounts of money involved, the quest for power became the real game played. Greed was a natural corollary. The Europeans could always tell their American critics, "Look, nearly all the monies and material for your railroad comes from Europe." They had a point.

Troubled by concerns over the manner in which London was handling securities, Reynolds decided to visit both McHenry and Salamanca. This was a dangerous mission during a war when Confederate commerce destroyers threatened Union shipping. In Spain, Salamanca expressed his disappointment with the slow progress in constructing the railroad. Understandably, the Civil War was a good explanation for the delay, with labor and supplies in short quantity, but the war also increased reluctance to invest in a country engaged in a political revolution.

Regardless, Salamanca insisted that his agreement with McHenry had called for the line by this time to have been completed to Akron, Ohio. It was not. McHenry was to furnish the funds, and then he (Salamanca) was to pay to finish the line to Dayton, Ohio. If McHenry could not comply with his agreement, Salamanca offered to fund the remaining construction with the understanding that he himself would be the managing contractor.

Whether the wine-and-dine treatment he had received in Europe softened his offensive strategy, Reynolds didn't say. Apparently, he had not been satisfied in London, for his sparring with McHenry and Kennard resumed upon his return to America. Not having ready cash to pay the bills on time remained a problem, as did that of recruiting labor. The choice of selecting workers now fell prey to the government, which was seeking more men for the military. The crisis forced the company to seek newly arrived immigrants. At least this source of labor was the cheapest form after slave labor.

The company hired many hundreds of Irish immigrants in addition to a number of Swedes, who spoke little, if any, English. To accommodate these workers, shanties were built along the line, where living conditions became deplorable. Immediately, sanitation, assimilation and communication issues created neighborhood unrest. Rival gangs of immigrant youngsters often clashed with children of permanent families. Sometimes the shenanigans and fighting carried over into the schools. It came as no surprise that many communities welcomed the eventual departure of these transients so that the shanties could be taken down and tranquility restored.

Nagging labor problems like these merely accentuated those of management. Aside from the persistent malady of meeting payroll, a serious crisis developed with a breakdown of trust between Reynolds and McHenry. It was a situation that could be resolved only when the relationship ended. Reynolds would have resigned sooner had it not been for his determination tó finish the job. The irony was that the construction went on, despite the friction between the two men. Additional branch lines were agreed to, and enough cash was gathered to compensate disgruntled workers before they stopped working. With physical signs of progress, Reynolds and Kent could only harbor their frustrations.

On June 20, 1864, the A&GW connected with the Cincinnati, Hamilton and Dayton Railroad at Dayton, to complete a broad-gauge line from New York City to St. Louis. Three months later, Reynolds and Kent resigned and returned to their business and civic pursuits.

At the time of their resignations, the future of the A&GW to them was tragically predictable, but not to the casual observer. He saw a different future for the company—anything but tragic. The main line from Salamanca, New York, to Dayton was complete—388 miles. In addition, there were 113 miles of branch lines. Thus, a total of 501 miles of line were built in thirty-eight months during a major war. This was quite an accomplishment. Why would the future be bleak?

Still, the publicity and glowing financial reports on the company reflected brightness from McHenry's manipulation of hidden mirrors. They represented more myth than reality. Faulty bookkeeping and misinformation only delayed the inevitable. The company began to default in its interest payments, creditors sued and the company finally went into receivership. A host of other problems plagued the company until 1880, when it was finally sold and reorganized as the New York, Pennsylvania and Ohio Company (NYPANO Railroad). The line's gauge was changed from six feet to the standard four feet, eight and a half inches.

William Reynolds drove his railroad dream to reality in a time when rail transportation was popular, oil had to be transported and an ugly war had to be fought. The need was there, and both Reynolds and the A&GW benefited from it. With peace restored in 1865, the company faced unprecedented competition, unscrupulous rail barons, national expansion and a financial panic. It was a time for wise management; unfortunately, it was not there.

FLORA BEST HARRIS,
A MEADVILLE MISSIONARY

A former Meadville resident, Hiroshi Okamoto, once asked me if I knew of the missionary Flora Best Harris. I pleaded ignorance. "Well," he responded, a bit surprised, "she's very famous in Japan and she came from Meadville." Embarrassingly, after an immediate search, I had to affirm my friend's claim. Not only was Flora a missionary, but she was a poet, scholar and musician, as well.

Communities are quick to praise their departing sons and daughters who achieve fame and glory in business, politics, the military and athletics, and rightfully so. But too often we neglect to recognize those low-key individuals who excel in their fields and have made a name for themselves outside their own communities.

One of these individuals is the Christian missionary. No one in Western civilization has been held in higher esteem. Over the centuries, however, too many of them have suffered horrific deaths for bringing spiritual and physical comfort to the unfortunate. On the American frontier, for example, Jesuits, those black-robed friars, were often butchered by hostile tribes. And the French military did not hesitate to turn natives into headhunters in search of English Moravians in colonial Pennsylvania.

Still, in modern times, sentiment has been largely in favor of this messenger of God. When death came to John Livingstone, a Canadian businessman of wealth and standing, he was identified simply as the brother of the more famous missionary and explorer, Dr. David Livingstone. And who can forget the dedication and service of such notables as Dr. Albert Schweitzer and Mother Theresa?

Flora Best Harris. *Crawford County Historical Society.*

Pennsylvania's Last Frontier

Flora Best Harris grew up on Center Street in Meadville. Two of her sisters, Margaret Blanche and Mary Luella, became physicians. A brother, Wesley Bensen, became an attorney, was county district attorney and for years served as a trustee of Allegheny College. Early in life, Flora knew she wanted to somehow help those in need.

In 1873, she married Merriman C. Harris of Beallsville, Ohio, an Allegheny graduate. Flora then knew what her destiny would be. Four years earlier, at the age of twenty-three, her husband had been accepted into the Pittsburgh Conference of the Methodist Church. The couple soon sailed for Japan to begin their church work. They opened their mission at Hakodate, where Harris also served as the United States consul. Prior to the Civil War, President James Buchanan had sent another Harris, New York merchant Townsend Harris, to Japan as the first American consul.

Flora and the Reverend Harris were warmly received by the Japanese people. They traveled extensively and made many lasting friendships. Reverend Harris was appointed superintendent of the Japanese mission of the Pacific coast, and in 1904 he was elected bishop of Japan and Korea. Twice, he was honored by the emperor and was influential in the diplomacy between the United States and Japan.

One of the couple's protégés was Inazo Nitobe, who was baptized by Harris. He and Flora spent time discussing cultural differences and a subject of mutual interest, literature. The young man went on to Johns Hopkins University, taught at Brown University and later became president of the Imperial College, Tokyo. After World War I, Nitobe served as undersecretary general of the League of Nations. He wrote extensively, including a biography of Flora, a woman he never forgot.

Flora was not reluctant to use her pen, either. She contributed articles to the *Christian Advocate* , translated one of Japan's classics, *Tosanikki*, and wrote numerous hymns and poems. One of her hymns, "O 'Tis Glory" is still sung in Japan. A compilation of her poems, with Japanese translation, is in the Crawford County Historical Society. L.V. Graham, who introduced Flora's poems to American readers in 1913, wrote, "Beauty and tenderness, pathos and power are combined in her writings."

Kazo Uchimura, one of Japan's ablest religious leaders, commented:

The land of Yamato has had many lovers. Among them, and in the foremost place, must be mentioned the name of Flora Best

Harris, a frail American woman and a missionary, too. She was one of those whose "nine parts are spirit and only one part flesh"...I know of no one, not even a native-born Japanese, whose love of Japan was so deep and pure. I myself have learned how to love my country from her.

After a visit to family and friends in the United States, she returned to Japan, where she died and was buried beside an infant daughter at Aoyama Tomb Park in Tokoyo.

WHEN THE RAILROAD CAME
TO EAST FALLOWFIELD

Crawford County in the mid-nineteenth century was in the throes of great economic flux. The canal was on its way out, the railroad was on its way in and the oil boom was starting. Nowhere were these changes more prevalent than in those towns and townships on the rail line. And no better insight into the impact of those changes can be acquired than through the eyes of a contemporary living in East Fallowfield.

Glenroie McQueen was only a lad when all this happened. In December, his unpublished memoir, "My First Forty," was donated to the Crawford County Historical Society by his great-granddaughter, Ginni McQueen of Ohio. This is a fascinating recollection, filled with anecdotes, place names and childhood memories that give us a better understanding of the quality of life in a very rural area when the railroads arrived during the Civil War.

The coming of the railroad, wrote McQueen, "completely revolutionized the simple life hitherto lived in our community." This is hardly an exaggeration. Lifestyles changed as the entire community adjusted to the demands of the new transportation industry. The railroad passed near McQueen's home, just south of Evansburg (now Conneaut Lake Borough), and through his grandmother's farm. He and his brother watched the tracks laid, telegraph poles set and the wires stretched. With everything in place, most citizens anxiously waited to see their first locomotive with its funnel-shaped smokestack.

McQueen recalled:

> *I remember how we ran from one pole to another, pressing our ears close against the pole, and hearing the humming of the wire occasioned by the wind, we imagined the telegraph was trying to say Monday or Thursday, and we jumped to the conclusion that on the following Monday or Thursday the Engine would put in an appearance.*

To lay the track, the railroad company brought in about "500 wild Irishman"—direct from southern Ireland. It was customary for rail companies to use newly arrived immigrants for the backbreaking jobs. This was the cheapest form of manpower available. To accommodate these workers, the company built shanties not too distant from the McQueen home. The exact location of "Shanty Town," as it was called, still remains a mystery. But it probably stood a quarter mile northwest of the intersection of the railroad and Township Route 387.

The Irish were not the only immigrants imported. McQueen mentions a "whole colony of raw Swedes, not one of whom could speak a word of English," brought in to lay track near Titusville. He came across them while helping Jim McMichael drive a team into the oil region. The Swedes also lived in makeshift housing. They enjoyed themselves with song and dance and introduced the young McQueen to the art of using snuff. This peculiar habit was in sharp contrast to the tobacco chewing of the men and the pipe smoking of the women in his own neighborhood.

Nationality groups did not always mix well. Rival gangs of Irish youngsters often clashed with the children of established families on their way to the "McQueen" School (most likely this was, or became, the McIntyre School, which closed in 1926). The battles between the Mushrush clan and the Irish became legendary. Sometimes the shenanigans and the feuding carried over into the school. Even the teachers were victimized—something that is normally regarded as a modern-day phenomenon.

Following is McQueen's vivid description of teacher abuse:

> *I saw a group of grown boys, during school hours, suddenly pounce upon a young woman teacher, pinion her arms, abstract*

*a letter they wanted from the front of her dress, and then with
hugs and kisses attempt to restore her good humor. I saw a man
teacher of the school locked out of the school room for two or
three hours until the Dominie had time to make arrangements to
provide candy for the whole school.*

After his family had moved to Evansburg Station at Stony Point,
McQueen naturally went to another school. Only then did he realize
how little he had learned at the McQueen School. It had been all fun
and games. He blamed this upon the railroad. Its workers and their
children, in his opinion, proved socially disruptive. But a few teachers of
the old school, like Henrietta Starron and Lizzie and Caroline McIntyre,
he never forgot. They were dedicated women "who wore their lives out
teaching county schools." Some of them never married because their
would-be husbands were lost in the war.

McQueen remembers the war years well. Many young men used the
new rails to take them to battle and to return home—many in dilapidated
uniforms and "not a few little better than human wrecks." He recalls the
numerous "war parties" for the draftees and volunteers either home on
furlough or on their way back to Union camps. More young women than
men attended these gatherings. Singing, dancing and light refreshments
highlighted the affairs. One of the popular ballads ran like this:

*Brave boys are they, gone at their country's call;
And yet, and yet, we cannot forget, how many brave boys must fall.*

The railroad did not bring instant prosperity to East Fallowfield. For
most of the residents, prosperity never came. Like the railroaders, they
remained poor. Most of the workers purchased their supplies—groceries,
notions, patent medicines—from McQueen's father. He did a credit
business, and this led to ruin. His books showed outstanding debts totaling
$10,000. He disposed of the store and entered the lumber business, which
provided wood for the railroad. Many of McQueen's neighbors did the
same thing. Oak trees were cut into logs sixty feet long, for which the
railroad "paid a fancy price" to make sills for the passenger cars. And
since wood was the only fuel used in the first locomotive, there was big
demand for it. McQueen's father had good timberland, and in winter he

Stony Point in East Fallowfield. The township was one of the first in the county through which the A&GW Railroad passed. *Crawford County Historical Society.*

kept four to six husky men chopping wood for the railroad. McQueen says that before going to bed, these stalwart woodcutters walked a mile through the snow in their bare feet to toughen them!

McQueen associates a number of bad memories with the railroad. Accidents were common. One evening, a young man with too much to drink used the track to return home and walked into an oncoming train. On another occasion, a brakeman fell from a caboose and was dragged to his death. Mangled bodies were often carried to the McQueen home. These experiences left a lasting impression on the lad. He commented:

> *In these latter days, railroad companies will not employ drinking men, but in the early days of railroading there were no such restrictions, and braking on the railroad seemed to have a peculiar fascination for a reckless, drunken class of young men, hence there were many casualties.*

McQueen did not spend the rest of his life in the Fallowfield-Conneaut area. He moved to Meadville, where he continued his studies, graduating from Allegheny in 1882. He then went to Princeton Seminary to complete his ministerial studies. A successful career as a Presbyterian minister followed. In recognition of his dedication and achievement, Allegheny awarded him an honorary degree in 1892.

McQueen's is a good memoir. It helps fill in the gaps in our knowledge of East Fallowfield. In addition, it provides fresh information on Meadville and the Conneaut Lake area. To the historian, firsthand impressions like this are indispensable to a study of the county during the last century, when the railroad arrived.

MACBETH OR BUFFALO BILL'S WILD WEST SHOW?

Which of the above would you prefer to see? A Shakespeare tragedy or a menagerie of performing cowboys, Native Americans and animals? Your selection probably reflects your favorite kind of entertainment: highbrow or something that is light. While one is formal and traditionally taught in school, the other is simple, often commercialized and American in taste. Both are found in every modern community, and both are dependent on financial support.

Meadville always enjoyed a history of the traditional form. In its early years, the town was recognized as the "oasis of northwestern Pennsylvania," the "Athens" on the state's last frontier. It had an academy, a college, churches, libraries and a prominent newspaper.

Responsible for much of this, in addition to the town being the county seat and being home to learned men like Timothy Alden, Harm Huidekoper and Thomas Atkinson, was an economy that benefited from land sales and commerce. By 1850, however, the economy had stagnated due to a depressed real estate market, financial panics and a faltering canal system. When William Reynolds tried to bring the railroad to town, he had to seek venture capital in Europe because local funding was very limited.

The oil boom, the Civil War and the railroad helped turn things around. Each related to America's industrialization, and each demanded manpower and supportive manufacturing. For the next several decades, businesses grew along with Meadville's population, which went from two thousand in 1850 to ten thousand in 1900.

Many of the new arrivals were Irish, German and Italian immigrants, young people from farms and former slaves from the South. They provided the manual labor in the railroad yard, the shops and factories. As consumers, they demanded the products and gadgetry of the industrial age, as well as cheap entertainment.

For years, Meadville had escaped the social pains of the big city. It had retained its rural identity, but this had to change. Historian Sarah Gordon faults the railroad for having deflowered the innocence of small towns. Aided by trains, the urban sprawl of the nineteenth century absorbed nearby communities and quickly transformed their institutions and culture. In 1863, Meadville was still twelve hours by rail from Pittsburgh, a good stretch, but not far enough to avoid interaction. Railroad networking started to make Pennsylvania look like a gigantic spider web on the map.

The interaction with much larger communities meant economic gain for Meadville, which was welcomed, but the type of entertainment that

On the way to the circus. Like the county fair, the circus was always a major attraction, especially when it featured a Wild West show. *Crawford County Historical Society.*

came with it was another matter. A steady diet of silent films, vaudeville, sporting events, melodrama, minstrels and circuses raised the serious question of what impact this all had on the youth. Meadville's intellectual elite admitted that this "pop culture" addiction of the urban masses was exciting and sometimes witty, yet it was too often vulgar and un-Christian. This critical ambivalence pretty much mirrored the attitudes of the town's people.

Regardless, the workingman was not dissuaded from patronizing that which he could enjoy and afford. The melodrama was indeed bad theater, for instance, but it was easily understood and usually flavored with a social theme that resonated with the audience. The story line easily distinguished the good guys from the villains. Seeing *Macbeth* performed at the opera house at Chestnut and Water was just not the same. Besides, it was cheaper to watch a slapstick routine or a two-reel flick at the nickelodeon on Water Street than a drama imported from New York City.

An opera singer at the Academy Theater. The theater, which still stands, featured both heavy and light entertainment. *Crawford County Historical Society.*

Following the Civil War, the local "patrons of the arts" fought back by encouraging intellectual pursuits and cultivating traditions of refinement and hospitality. To that end, they started various organizations. The Library, Art and Historical Association; the Literary Union; and the Woman's Club were a few among them. They also brought in famous actors and singers, leading clergy speakers, noted artists and musicians. And they promoted literary publications like *The Chautauquan*. The circus might still retain top billing of all entertainment, but it could never bury the enthusiasm and support for the legitimate theater, a Mozart concert or an art exhibit.

Who were these enlightened people? They came from all fields—law, business, education, publishing, ministry, etc. To mention a few: William Reynolds, Ernest Hempstead, Theodore Flood, Ida Tarbell, George and Charles Haskins and Samuel Bates. Along with the faculties of Allegheny College and the Theological School, they became the custodians of what they valued as a culture worth saving. In their opinion, to overindulge in the more popular forms of fun was to engage in cultural masochism.

Did this point to a community cleavage between the very literate and everyone else? Perhaps. Author Frederic Howe came close to suggesting this when he alluded to the social layers of Meadville he remembered. He recalled being forbidden to mix with other youth across the tracks to attend one of those trashy productions. But Howe belonged to the Progressive movement that demanded, after 1900, wholesale reforms. In effect, he was still rebelling against a society that, for him as a young man, had refused to modernize.

If this cultural conflict did indeed exist, it caused no permanent damage in our community or, for that matter, in any other. Professors enjoyed, and still enjoy, going to a sporting event and taking their children to the circus. And "blue-collar" families of every generation continue to believe that their children must go to school and study Shakespeare or Italian Renaissance because education is the way to the future. Most of us see the value of both recreation and structured learning. Ideally, we see a healthy balance of the two for our young people. "Have fun," we tell them. "Play your video games, but don't neglect your books."

FOUR WOMEN
WHO MADE A DIFFERENCE

There have been many talented and enlightened women with roots in Crawford County. Four of them are remembered for their creative achievements. All found ways to express themselves as original thinkers and social doers despite tradition that would have relegated them to the long-accepted female roles of teacher, nun and dutiful housewife.

The humanitarianism of two of these women led to the start of Meadville's two hospitals. During the Civil War, the former Spencer Hospital opened as an asylum for orphaned children. When a local train wreck in 1869 resulted in many injuries, an appeal went out to the Sisters of St. Joseph, who operated the asylum, to care for the victims. Their immediate offer to help resulted in a move to establish a much-needed hospital in a town whose population was on the increase.

The following year, St. Joseph's Hospital was organized, with Mother Agnes Spencer in charge and seven other sisters to assist her. Under her leadership, the number of admissions steadily rose. As the facility continued to expand its services, additional nurses and staff were required. In 1888, the hospital's name was changed to Spencer Hospital in memory of its founder.

In the same spirit as Mother Agnes Spencer, Nancy Northam turned her compassion to the poor and destitute. Just as the community had asked the St. Joseph Sisters to help, so Nancy Northam asked the community for a place where those in need and the ill could find care. She helped prompt a gathering of civic leaders at the county courthouse to explore the possibility of such a place.

Mother Agnes Spencer. *Crawford County Historical Society.*

She was persuasive, and her arguments evidently proved sound, for the town leaders could not reject her plea. In July 1880, a number of them, including Joshua Douglas and Reverend Richard Craighead, organized themselves as directors of a city hospital to care for the sick and the aged. Shortly afterward, they appointed a ladies advisory committee, a significant development that further illustrated the changing role of women in the male-dominated society of the nineteenth century. Property at the bottom of Highland Avenue was purchased for construction of the hospital. The first patient in 1881 was a veteran of the War of 1812.

Another woman of limitless drive, insight and dedication to social causes was Josephine Brawley Hughes. Perhaps more than any other woman from the Meadville area, Josephine demonstrated to the skeptics that a woman can have enormous power to influence public opinion. Born outside of Meadville, she attended Edinboro State Normal, where she met her future husband, Lewis C. Hughes. Upon graduation, she taught school and he studied law in the offices of Brawley and Derickson. In 1870, the couple was married in Meadville's First Presbyterian Church.

This young woman was tough enough to brave the challenge of the frontier of the Arizona Territory. She joined her husband after he had moved there for health reasons. She climbed off the stage in Tucson, allegedly carrying a rifle and a baby daughter. A dusty village of adobe buildings with dirt floors greeted her. Renegades, swashbuckling gunslingers and hostile Apaches added to the nightmare. Only the cacti, lizards and Gila monsters seemed at home in the boundless wilderness.

By our standards, Josephine and Lewis had to be radicals, if not militants. Recognizing the power of the press to bring about change, they started the first daily paper in Arizona, the *Tucson Daily Star*. It soon became the mouthpiece of reform, a beacon for churches and civic organizations fighting against those "evil influences." Gambling houses and saloons were continually and mercilessly attacked until many of them closed.

Josephine Hughes also directed her passions toward institutional development and civil rights. She believed they were vital to any social progress. When Lewis was appointed territorial governor in 1893, he was able to strengthen her crusade. She established the first girls' school and taught classes herself. She led in the organization of Methodism in Tucson, a spiritual force for reform. Along with Frances Willard, a

Alice Bentley. *Crawford County Historical Society.*

close friend, Josephine crusaded for temperance and organized the first Women's Christian Temperance Union (WCTU). When she took up the suffrage cause, another close friend, Susan B. Anthony, helped.

Josephine became legendary. Called "the Mother of Arizona," a memorial in her honor is in the rotunda of the statehouse in Phoenix. The inscription reads:

> *Erected to the memory of Mrs. E. Josephine Brawley Hughes, wife of Lewis C. Hughes, Governor of Arizona, Mother of Methodism in Arizona, and Founder of the W.C.T.U. in Arizona. Founder of the first daily newspaper in Arizona. Born December 22, 1839 near Meadville, PA. Died April 22, 1926.*

Mother Agnes Spencer, Nancy Northam and Josephine Hughes best represented the reform movement in the decades following the Civil War. It was an age of industrialization, urbanization and further development of the West. All through these changes, the American woman was beginning to play a larger role in fashioning the new society. She recognized and easily identified with the problems of the time—poverty, inadequate housing, mental illness, illiteracy, inequalities, etc. For the first time, she narrowed the gender gap as she assumed more of a leadership role in addressing these problems.

One local woman who rode the wave of social achievements by earlier women was Alice M. Bentley, one of the first women elected to the Pennsylvania General Assembly. After graduating from Edinboro State Normal School, she taught elementary classes in Guys Mills and Meadville. After a time with an insurance company, she ran for the General Assembly in 1922. Gaining support from educators and business leaders, she won and served from 1923 to 1928. She became the first woman to serve as Speaker of the House.

Like the suffragists, Alice Bentley believed that women voting and serving in public office could only make the political system better. She disliked party bosses and only wanted to be the spokesperson for the masses.

Each of these four women helped the women of the next generation make further progress. They were interested not only in closing the so-called gender gap, but also addressing social problems that were very much related to the family: decent housing, education, child abuse, drugs, alcoholism, child pornography and prostitution, etc. All of these touched the family and thus were of primary concern to women.

The cheap melodrama of the early twentieth century seems to offer a farcical yet serious perspective and relevancy. The scene has a poor young woman feeding her children. They're both in raggedy clothes. The food is spotty, and the room is less than homey. The woman is distressed. She keeps looking at the clock. Where is her husband? She knows where he always is on payday. He's at the saloon. A knock at the door. A gaunt-looking man dressed in black enters. The villain! The audience hisses. The landlord has come for the rent, which is due now, and the poor woman doesn't have it. He threatens to throw them out, but before he leaves, he leers at the fifteen-year-old daughter and whispers something in the mother's ear. The audience knows what he probably said. The woman shows panic and falls to her knees, begging the landlord for more time. He shakes his head. The curtain falls on the first scene. Many of the day's social problems were dramatized in that one scene. The reform-minded women in the audience believed that it was time for change and pledged to do something to bring about that change.

TO SAVE OR NOT TO SAVE?

I finally finished the annual chore of cleaning my shed. Moving items back and forth, I must have asked myself a dozen times, "Why am I keeping this?" All of us ask the same question every time we attack those chambers of horror—the garage, attic, basement or shed.

Wondering whether something should be saved or consigned to the bottomless dumpster confronts everyone. Living in a society that leads the world in trash, we may assume that we are ditching and bulldozing more than we are keeping. But are we? Some economist may have concocted an equation that correlates, in a grand sweep, productivity, consumption, preservation and waste. It might even tell us what we have been doing right and what we have been doing wrong. If such a mathematical contrivance already exists, I have forgotten it.

So what is worth saving? Recently, a librarian in New Mexico discovered a small envelope buried in an 1888 book on Civil War medicine. The inscription on the envelope read, "Scabs from vaccination of W. B. Yarrington's children." It was signed by the doctor who had authored the book. Apparently the good doctor believed that the scabs needed to be saved.

The envelope and its ghastly contents created an immediate stir in the science community. At present, they are in a freezer at the Centers for Disease Control and Prevention in Atlanta. Whatever researchers uncover may shed light on the development of American vaccines for smallpox. There is also the slight chance that the scabs could provide information leading to a better understanding of the evolutionary nature of the disease.

The county courthouse. *Crawford County Historical Society.*

Pennsylvania's Last Frontier

As a historian, I may wish to keep everything that informs me of the past. The archaeologist and paleontologist may have a similar wish. Yet this is impractical. What sensible rules or guidelines can these professionals adopt that can serve their sciences and the public without laying undue stress on the taxpayer with too many museums, zoological and botanical gardens and archival centers?

For discussion, we can break down the saving game four ways, excluding that which is being done to save lives. We can keep something that has personal worth, monetary value or legal or historical significance. There can be other categories, but the four mentioned are a good start.

Imagine seeing a distraught woman standing in front of what used to be her home, which was recently ravaged by a tornado. Holding a family album, she tells a reporter that the most important thing to her—the album—was miraculously saved. Her tragic comment illustrates a good example of personal worth. Individuals are generally not apt to relinquish family Bibles, heirlooms and photos. Their grandchildren may, however.

Many articles can bring money, as well. Just how much is grandpap's watch or stamp collection worth? A reputable collector or an excursion on eBay could provide an answer. Markets determine monetary value. Some articles appreciate over time; others do not. Once its market value goes down, an article generally loses its appeal and, unless it still has personal worth, becomes a feature at a flea market or rummage sale.

Third, all levels of government maintain records. The law requires that certain materials be kept for at least a period of time. Some are centuries old. As government functions increase, so does the paperwork; city halls and courthouses are clogged with it. Those records that can be legally disposed of are often given to a local historical society or museum. Microfilming has helped, but this is expensive. Most Pennsylvania counties have records management programs and have either built repositories or converted structures to house community documents of every kind. Crawford County does not have such a facility, but its courthouse does serve as a repository.

Finally, what is historically significant? Maybe a bridge or train depot? Professionals and government experts can help make that determination. Yet how many old structures can be preserved without state and federal assistance? For a community with a shortage of benefactors, the answer is probably not too many. Hard decisions are based on monies available and the community's priorities.

Baldwin-Reynolds Icehouse. *Crawford County Historical Society.*

Preserving old documents, such as early maps or someone's letters, is similar to that of keeping a historic building. Both deal with something of local or regional interest, except for a document of national importance. A document that has neither a local nor national connection is generally not accepted by a county historical society and most likely will be destroyed by its owner. This is unfortunate—a good deal of paper history is lost this way. But societies have limited space and too few staff who can spend time looking for a proper home for a particular document.

So the next time you are cleaning the attic and cannot decide whether to keep an item, ask yourself the following: Does this still mean that much to me or my family? Can I sell it for a few bucks? Could it have legal import without being a missing murder weapon? And might it possibly change our perception of some great event in history? Like me, you may not be able to answer this litany of questions. You will then put the item back in the corner and await next year's cleaning.

CRAWFORD COUNTY'S WORKINGMEN AND FARMERS REBELLED IN 1896

For journalist Lynam Frank Baum, creator of *The Wonderful Wizard of Oz*, the escape from the harsh realities of farm life into a world of fantasy was often necessary. Other authors also recorded the endless drudgery of caring for the land against tornados, floods, droughts, unfair railroad barons and the poverty that methodically smothered the best of dreams.

These writers represented Populism, which swept across much of America in the late nineteenth century. Before it was through, it had recruited millions of struggling farmers and workingmen, as well. This reform movement stressed two points: people, and not the plutocrats, must control the government, and the government must restrain the greedy few who profit at the expense of the poor.

Who were the county Populists, and what was their agenda? Only a few can be mentioned: Walter Tucker of Cambridge Springs, Curtis S. Clark of Meadville, Alfred Nunn of Mead, E.T. Mason of Conneautville and C.A. Stranahan of Sparta. They wanted equal rights; an increase in money supply; free coinage of silver; direct election of top officials, including the president and U.S. senators; a crackdown on monopolies; a graduated income tax; and government ownership of railroads and public utilities. Some of these were eventually adopted; some were not. Two local newspapers supported the Populist cause: the *Pennsylvania Farmer* and the *People's Advocate and Sledge-Hammer*.

The demands nudged the county as far to the political left as any previous set of reforms. In fact, they reeked too much of socialism to suit the establishment and political traditionalists. Fear of the Populists grew from a set of confused values of the present and doubts of the future. The 1890s was a decade of boom and bust, general bewilderment and distraction. Industrial expansion, imperialism, financial panic, increased immigration and many other problems jolted Americans into sensing that their country was changing, and not necessarily for the better.

The Populist Ignatius Donnelly saw all this anxiety and confusion to be the result of class conflicts by gross injustice in the economic order. He summed it up this way: unscrupulous capitalists and an accommodating government were breeding two classes, millionaires and tramps. Populist candidate for county district attorney, Philip Willet, gave a throng at the courthouse and Diamond Park the same message: "Party lines are obliterated and the contest [election of 1896] is of the masses against the classes."

In that year, national and local Populists joined the Democrats in a fusion the Republicans jeeringly called "Popocracy." But the laugh was on the Republicans. Election results for the county stunned nearly everyone. While the fusion candidate for president, William J. Bryan, lost the national race to William McKinley, he won locally. This was a real blow to Republicans who had carried the county with their presidential standard-bearer since John C. Freemont in 1856. The fusion candidate for Congress, Joseph Sibley of Franklin, also won in the county, as did three fusionists for the General Assembly. How embarrassing it must have been for the nearly seven hundred Crawford Republicans who made the pilgrimage to Canton, Ohio, to assure McKinley of the county's total support.

Voting patterns were similar to those that had occurred in the time of Andrew Jackson. Blue-collar workers from Titusville and the Third and Fourth Wards of Meadville joined with angry farmers to support the fusionists. Poverty over privilege? Perhaps. At least there is some good evidence. In the Fourth Ward, for example, one half (526) of the taxpayers paid the minimal tax of fifteen cents for the tax year 1895. Many of these were Irish, Italian and German immigrants who were grubbing out a living on the railroad or in some factory.

In contrast, the per capita tax averaged $5.55 for the First Ward, which heavily voted for McKinley. In 1900, the Third and Fourth Wards again voted for Bryan, but McKinley squeaked by to a county victory.

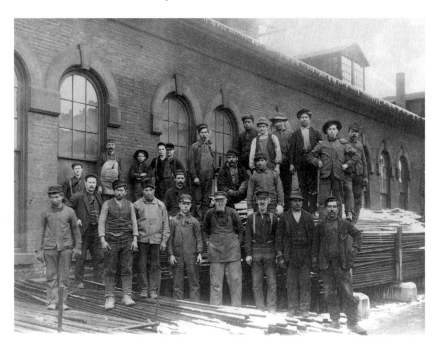

Workers at the Erie Railroad Foundry. County blue-collar workers were becoming politically active by the late nineteenth century. *Crawford County Historical Society.*

Admittedly, the workingman was in the pits, but no more than the farmer. The latter's grin-and-bear-it philosophy, the product of centuries of dedication to the soil and a legacy of fair play, seemed out of step with modern America. His defense of everything that was spiritually correct and socially sound now appeared defenseless. Yet his pride remained unbroken.

Most county farmers had joined the party of Lincoln because they saw in the new republicanism a fresh hope. It offered sensible balance between fulfilling the nation's economic needs and providing a humane approach to the downtrodden masses, including the slave, the freedman, the factory worker and the farmer. Now, in 1896, there was the question of what Lincoln's party stood for. The Populist creed looked as attractive now as the Republican program had forty years earlier.

The farmer was sure of one thing: the market. Farm prices, which had been on the decline since the 1860s, touched bottom in the 1890s. In Kansas and Nebraska, it was cheaper to burn wheat and corn than to sell it. Writing in her diary in the 1890s, Marion Finney Canfield, of Cambridge Springs, recorded the realities of agricultural economics. She quoted many prices. The eggs she delivered to market for fourteen cents a dozen sold for seventeen cents twenty years earlier. In 1892, corn was fifty cents a bushel; four years later it dropped to twenty-eight cents. Potatoes were seventy cents in 1892; in 1896, they were twenty cents and so forth.

Fortunately, the farmers and the workingmen in 1896 rebelled with the ballot and not with pitchforks and sledgehammers. Their victory was nominal. They lacked the staying power of the early Republicans or Jacksonians before them. Yet they proved that peaceful change is possible if the protest is loud enough and the voters get out.

Still, even today, with retention among elected officials running about 90 percent, throwing out the entrenched incumbents is not easy. Voters realize this and, thus, as many as 50 or 60 percent do not bother to vote. How unfortunate. There may be a correlation between retention rate and voter turnout, but I'll leave that to the political scientist to explain.

LOCAL AUTHORS STOOD OUT IN PROGRESSIVE MOVEMENT

The Progressive movement in America at the beginning of the twentieth century had some of its roots in the previous century. It drew its energy from the Populist agitation of the 1890s, the discontent of the urban masses and the general disgust with political and business leaders. The passion for reform received a sympathetic nod from the presidencies of Theodore Roosevelt, William Howard Taft and Woodrow Wilson, during which time considerable social progress was made.

Writers shared credit for much of this progress. Popular-priced magazines with wide circulation, like *McClure's Magazine*, featured articles that described and often sensationalized abuses and wrongdoings in the nation's economic and political systems. This was an age of investigative reporting, with writers using research skills to get to the heart of a story. Many reputations were bruised by these literary assaults. "Muckraking," as the process was called, extended even to fiction. One fine example was Upton Sinclair's novel *The Jungle* (1906), which dealt with the meatpacking industry and its callous disregard for the health of the consumer.

Two local authors attained notoriety in this age of reform. As with most Progressives, their interests and contributions varied, which suggested the span of problems the nation faced. Frederic Howe (1867–1940) grew up in Meadville, where, as he wrote in *The Confessions of a Reformer* (1925), stifling orthodoxy was the norm. Allegheny College, with its Methodism, and the Meadville Theological School, with its Unitarianism, were the twin bastions of orthodoxy that symbolized the intellectual strength of the community, while the evangelical morality of duty glued the community.

Frederic C. Howe. *Crawford County Historical Society.*

Howe graduated from Allegheny College and completed his formal education at Johns Hopkins in Baltimore. He loved the excitement of the big city. In Cleveland, he joined a law firm and also became active in charitable organizations. He fell under the influence of Tom Johnson, perhaps the most successful urban reformer of his day. Howe was elected to city council in 1901, the same year that Johnson was elected mayor.

Howe believed in information and organized intelligence to transform both society and government. Good leadership was essential. He would be in total ecstasy in today's computer age. In *The City: The Hope of Democracy* (1905), he despaired over the city with its diseases, infant mortality, poverty and inadequate housing. He believed there was no reason why the city could not be beautiful, cultured, hospitable and humane to its citizens. Two years later, he wrote *The British City: The Beginnings of Democracy.*

From Cleveland, Howe moved to New York City, where he became commissioner of immigration at Ellis Island. It was the World War I era, a time of strong anti-immigrant feeling in the country. Howe worked hard to prevent needless deportations. After the war, he attended the Paris Peace Conference. During this time, his politics changed. When he ran for city council in Cleveland, he ran as a Republican. Since the beginning of the war, he assumed more of a liberal position and called for more reform. In the 1932 election, he supported F.D. Roosevelt and later served as consumer's counsel in the Agricultural Adjustment Administration. He also became special adviser to Secretary of Agriculture Henry Wallace. After his death in 1940, he was buried in Meadville, the city he had found as a youth to be too conventional.

A contemporary of Howe's who also stood out in the Progressive period was Ida Tarbell (1857–1944). Born in Erie County, she moved with her parents to the oil region around Titusville, Crawford County, at an early age. Growing up in the shadows of countless derricks, she witnessed both the good and the bad of an industry that affected so many lives. She listened to her father, who was an oil tank manufacturer, speak openly against the Standard Oil Company for its unfair practices. His criticism may or may not have triggered a passion in his daughter to someday record the injustices and inequities he had suffered.

Ida Tarbell also graduated from Allegheny College and taught school for a few years in Ohio. When she was offered to do some writing for *The Chautauquan*, a magazine published in Meadville, she accepted and

Ida M. Tarbell. *Crawford County Historical Society.*

IN THE FOOTSTEPS
of
LINCOLN
BY IDA M. TARBELL

COMPLIMENTS OF THE
BUFFALO EVENING NEWS

A Lincoln biography. This work by Ida Tarbell helped advance her literary career.
Crawford County Historical Society.

remained with the publication for several years. Writing biography interested her. She went to France, where she met writers and got inspired to write biographies of Napoleon Bonaparte and Madame Roland, a supporter of republicanism during the French Revolution. As fine as these studies were, she attained national recognition with her work on Abraham Lincoln.

A turning point in Tarbell's career occurred in 1894, when S.S. McClure asked her to write material for *McClure's Magazine*, which he had founded the previous year. Its low price and "muckraking" articles made it one of the nation's top publications. McClure succeeded in also recruiting the talents of Lincoln Steffens, who wrote on municipal corruption, and Ray S. Baker, another fact-finder, who examined labor relations and railroad rates. McClure asked Tarbell to do a study of John D. Rockefeller of Standard Oil. Over a five-year period, she applied research skills to uncover what she could to produce articles acknowledging Rockefeller's brilliance and ruthlessness. Business espionage, conspiracy against competitors and manipulation of railroad rates to benefit the trust he had created resulted in Rockefeller becoming the most celebrated businessman to be victimized by investigative reporting.

What Tarbell had written on Standard Oil led the U.S. Supreme Court in 1911 to rule that the company had violated the Sherman Antitrust Act and had to be dissolved. This was a personal victory for her, perhaps to match the severity of the damage to her father and other oilmen. Yet a larger victory belonged to a vigilant press that continued to expose misbehavior by America's leading industrialists. Tarbell continued to write and lecture on the art of biographical history. She also expressed an interest in the peace movement and the social role of women. With other Progressives, she hoped to see her age remembered as one of significant reform in American society. This could happen only with government help, for she had learned that the business community lacked the instinct or desire to cleanse itself. She believed in a "socialized democracy," unlike some of the muckrakers who turned to socialism.

GONE INDUSTRIES
THAT WERE SO UNIQUE

Crawford County has had a long tradition of being a manufacturing center in a rural setting. Most of our factories and shops have fallen into the category of being typical; that is, the likes of which you can find in most counties of comparable size and population. While the tool industry has been present and consistently dominant for a century, the five businesses in this essay illustrate the diversity of county productivity. They stood out in their time but are no longer with us. And they were different because of what they did.

Shadeland has always been one of my favorites. Thomas Jefferson, a great supporter of agriculture, would have been proud of this stock farm. The Powell family operated the farm in Spring Township for more than a half century. By the 1850s, it already had the reputation of being one of the better stock farms in the region. Watkin Powell had moved his family from the Mohawk Valley of New York. His three sons (Watkin Jr., William and James) helped make Shadeland world famous.

Their sales were phenomenal. The family's business records at the county historical society document the fantastic story. The brothers sold thousands of horses to individuals and stock dealers. Prices ranged from as little as fifty dollars to many thousands. Customers included Buffalo Bill Cody, the Prince of Wales and the Japanese royal family. It is said that the Powell brothers had more of their horses registered than any five similar farms in the world combined.

Hambleton racers and trotters were among the more popular horses. This particular breed was named after the famous trotter Hambletonian

10, and from this horse the lineage of American Standardbred racehorses can be traced. At Shadeland, trotters were exercised and trained on a special track along Conneaut Creek. Famed horses were sometimes buried along the creek and honored with different trees.

Other breeds included the Hackney, Clydesdale and Morgan. The Morgan was noted for its versatility. It was the horse used by the pony express and U.S. Cavalry. Many of them found action in the Civil War. The Powells also sold Shetland and Welsh ponies.

The farm also bred cattle, sheep and swine. Unknown to most people, a special area was set aside for the preservation of game—elk, buffalo, antelope and bear—just to mention a few. Why this was done, the records don't explain.

Like other business ventures affected by a new turn in technology, so Shadeland's breeding establishment drew to a close with the advent of the automobile. Eventually, the property was sold to St. Sava's Serbian Orthodox Church in Pittsburgh and used as a charity home. In 1992, the church had the home burned.

Not far from Shadeland was another interesting business, this one organized by L.C. Graves of Springboro. He was a blacksmith who decided in the 1880s to build wagons, sleighs and carriages. These were good market items in a time when most people traveled or hauled goods over short distances. After a devastating fire had destroyed his initial building, Graves raised the capital to build two sturdier buildings and promised to fill them with dozens of workers.

Sales took off. Many of the carriages and buggies were shipped to distant markets on the Bessemer and Lake Erie Railroad. The L.C. Graves Company became one of the more enterprising firms in the western regions of the county. More workers had to be added and a freight shed constructed. Anyone who had special skills either as a carpenter or metal worker was in big demand. Legend indicates that employment was guaranteed for three years for some workers, but I have no documentary evidence to support that claim.

Like Shadeland, the company at the time of World War I found the automobile to be a serious challenge. The company's assets were sold, and the plant was converted from manufacturing carriages and sleighs to making parts for Ford Motor.

This typical and sad ending does fortunately have a happy side. Faith Scott of Springboro wrote a fine article for the historical society's newsletter and included a number of passages from letters of those who had bought one of the company's products. The owners expressed their pleasure with what they had and treasured them as precious collectibles, which they are. I just wonder how many products of the L.C. Graves Company still exist.

The automobile may have hastened the demise of both Shadeland and the carriage business of L.C. Graves, but it found a friend in the Keystone View Company of Meadville. Many auto drivers who experienced difficulty seeing when behind the wheel benefited from the eye-corrective exercises produced by this firm. These products represented but a fraction of the total number of different items sold by Keystone View in its nearly eighty years of doing business.

The company was founded in 1892 by B.L. Singley. He had been a salesperson for Underwood & Underwood, another distributor of stereographic images. This kind of photography that combines images of two pictures taken from different angles, thus producing a three-dimensional effect, had become extremely popular by the end of the nineteenth century. Singley's company immediately began to file for patents and to purchase negative collections.

By the 1920s, Keystone View became one of the larger, if not the largest, distributor of stereographs and stereographic equipment. At that

The Keystone View Company in Meadville. *Crawford County Historical Society.*

time, three-dimensional imaging worked its way into movie production. The "golden age" of 3-D movies erupted in the 1950s, with Polaroid filters, those funny disposable anaglyph glasses made of cardboard and stereophonic sound.

Keystone's stereographs covered many subjects—faraway places, American cities and towns, technology and Native Americans. They sold in sets housed in slip-case boxes. When placed side by side in a bookcase, the boxes looked like books. A number of these are at the historical society in Meadville. Also included in the society's collections are illustrative literature and catalogues of the company. Were these items expensive? Relatively speaking, they were. Views sold for a little more than sixteen cents each, and viewers went for about ninety cents. The Johnson-Shaw Museum in Meadville displays original Keystone equipment and views.

In 1963, Keystone View was acquired by the Mast Company. It ceased operations in the 1970s. In 1978, Keystone's gigantic collection consisting

Workers at Keystone Ordnance Works in the TNT department. The risk of a cataclysmic disaster at this munitions plant was always present. *Crawford County Historical Society.*

of business papers and negatives was donated to the UCR/California Museum of Photography at the University of California Riverside. When I asked why some institution like the historical society or Allegheny College did not try to corral this significant collection, the answer given was, "Where can you put thirty tons of stuff?"

If thirty tons of the Keystone View collection seemed a great deal to store, what about storing trinitrotoluene—also called TNT—weighing considerably more? The federal government faced this problem when it built a munitions plant during World War II in Greenwood Township, Crawford County. The Keystone Ordnance Works (KOW) became the largest manufacturing complex ever built in the county. Its five hundred or so structures dotted the landscape of fourteen thousand acres or twenty-two square miles. It was one of those "war babies" created in response to Japan's attack on Pearl Harbor.

Obviously, the new plant brought in thousands of jobs. At the time of its closing at the end of the war, KOW employed 1,650 workers—scientists, technicians, medical staff, security specialists, maintenance and office personnel. Federal employment meant probable deferment from military service, decent wages and benefits and steady work until the war ended. Buses transported workers from nearby communities.

The downside to the operation was the dislocation and hardship of hundreds of residents who had to evacuate their homes and farms. They had been offered what the government considered to be fair prices for their properties. Many, perhaps most, believed the purchase price of the typical farm was not fair. The residents could hardly negotiate with officials. They knew the government was exercising the right of eminent domain—seizing private property in public interest. Besides, this was war, and who said war was fun or fair? Thirty years after the event, some residents who had been dispossessed still didn't care to talk about it with researchers.

TNT is something you don't play with. KOW officials took every precaution to make sure a cataclysmic accident did not occur. Explosives were stored in concrete magazines, set comfortably apart from one another. Some one hundred of these "igloos" were still used decades after the war as homes for a number of families. From the time it began operation in September 1942 to the end of the war, the KOW produced about 250,000,000 pounds of explosives.

Talon workers. *Crawford County Historical Society.*

In the late 1940s, the government began to disassemble the plant. The price tag for the entire layout was $53,000,000, but who was in the market for a munitions plant other than, perhaps, some terrorist group? Some things were sold, some buildings and equipment were given away and many structures were demolished. By the 1970s, serious questions arose regarding toxic residue, disposal of waste and buried metal drums that had held chemicals or fuels. When I asked a woman who had worked in the chemical division what happened to the waste materials, she simply answered, "Why, we just dumped it on the ground."

The one company that could challenge KOW's exemplary record of job creation was Talon, Inc. of Meadville. Unlike the munitions plant that manufactured TNT for a brief period, Talon consistently made products the world wanted over a period of eighty years. In 1941, the company furnished 5,219 of the city's 9,000 industrial jobs. Its sales that year reached $30,000,000, with a profit of $5,000,000. The company had the greatest impact on the county's industrial history.

A beauty queen in a zipper outfit. This definitely demonstrates the versatility of the zipper. *Crawford County Historical Society.*

In 1913, Colonel Lewis Walker started the company in a red barn on Race Street. In 1937, the name was changed from Hookless Fastener to Talon, Inc. Walker brought in a Swedish-born engineer, Gideon Sundback, who would invent the first version of the zipper based on interlocking teeth. This was the "Hookless Fastener No. 2." Its predecessor, "Hookless Fastener No. 1," had design defects that made it less than a commercial success. Sundback's version made it an instant triumph.

B.F. Goodrich coined the term "zipper" in 1923 for a line of its rubber overshoes, or arctics. In this decade, Hookless Fastener netted most of its profits from steady business with Goodrich for zippers on items like arctics and tobacco pouches. Its second-best customer may have been H.D. Lee Mercantile Company, which made overalls and outfits for firemen. By then, slide fasteners started to appear on vacuum cleaner bags, school bags, hunting boots, children's leggings, men's trousers and jackets and, finally, women's apparel.

World War II led to numerous government contracts, but it also created for manufacturers a shortage of precious metals, including copper. While this spelled disaster for some smaller companies, Talon used its resources and inventiveness to produce a zinc-on-steel fastener identified by the letter v—v for victory.

Yet the fastener was not enough. Talon's engineers had to design new machinery to manufacture military products the government required. These included mine detectors, parts for antiaircraft weapons, grease cups for rifles and bomb and shell fuses. The company purchased Electroweld Steel Corporation of Oil City, which made shell containers. Also for the war effort, Talon diversified more by making plastic zippers, plastic poker chips and other plastic items.

After the war, Talon continued to devise new ways of doing things by creating new products. Some of this called for starting new plants nationally. Some were opened at Morton, Mississippi and Cleveland, Georgia. At its plant at Woodland, North Carolina, Talon introduced a new fastener design to compete with low-priced fasteners used in women's clothes. Called the Falcon, it became a market favorite. At Stanley, North Carolina, a tape and cord manufacturing plant with dyeing capabilities was established.

New plants, additional acquisitions and different products characterized Talon's growth and diversification over the recent decades. A fastener, called Big-Zip, was primarily made for men's and boys' jackets. It was popular because of its "rugged" character. The introduction of the Zephyr in 1960 was another milestone for the company. This item was different from all others for it was made of nylon filament, had no metal scoops and the slider moved smoothly. With the Zephyr, Talon's sales reached a new all-time high for the company.

Talon's success story resulted from visionary executives like Colonel Walker and Lewis Walker III, brilliant engineering, healthy labor relations, an apprenticeship program that enabled some workers eventually to start their own businesses and a good relationship with the community.

Each of these five enterprises, different from one another, created something that was needed by many, many people. Whether it was a carriage or a ton of TNT, it was done with extraordinary skill and leadership. Singularly, their histories are unique, but collectively they tell some of the story of Crawford County's economic excellence from the standpoint of some of its diverse industries.

"A TOOL! A TOOL! MY KINGDOM FOR A TOOL!"

Was the title above the frantic cry of King Richard III? Of course not, but it could have been the frantic cry of an early settler in Crawford County. His desperate need for tools matched his wife's for a kettle and kitchen utensils.

Once I asked my freshman class in American history what most important device would they take to the frontier of western Pennsylvania? I received some thoughtful comments. One young man said a rifle to protect his family and hunt for food; another said an axe to fell trees for a cabin; a third answered that neither a rifle nor an axe was useful if he could not transport his family, so he opted for a good wagon, assuming he had a horse or a team of oxen to pull it. Finally, a young woman grimaced and quipped, "I'd take paper and whatever they used back then to write with, to tell my mother back home how dumb I was to let my husband talk me into coming to this godforsaken wilderness!"

So much for technology and the westward movement: progress is always in the eye of the beholder. If we relate progress to technological advances, we may have trouble convincing everyone. Inventions are not always appreciated at the time of their creation. Skeptics and pessimists tend to be blinded by the downside of anything new. At first I was not keen on automatic transmission, color television or contact lenses, but eventually I came around like everyone else. Once capitalism sees and improves the product's marketability, the public mood generally changes and the product becomes mainstream. We see this all the time.

The pioneer hardly quibbled over a product's possible downside. If a new tool was functional and affordable, he wanted it. And that was the problem. Most of the settlers did not bring all the tools they would need to start a new life, and the tools they needed were not always immediately available. When they became available, the settler didn't always have the money to purchase them.

Crawford County had a long way to go to achieve the reputation of being a manufacturing center. Hardware of any kind had to be imported from places like Pittsburgh and Philadelphia at high cost. By 1812, freight from Philadelphia to Meadville averaged from six to nine dollars per hundred pounds—a lot of money back then for those struggling on hardscrabble farms. Thus, borrowing tools from one's neighbor, after having borrowed his oxen to plow a field, became commonplace. Sharing and bartering were powerful forces among our first settlers.

Those who had purchased their land from one of the land companies, like the Holland Land or Pennsylvania Population, enjoyed one advantage. Backed by Eastern and European capitalists, these companies operated as businesses, with profit as the goal. They tried to accommodate their settlers the best they could by bringing in crucial goods, including tools, establishing stores, and building roads, sawmills and gristmills. Satisfying their settlers meant attracting other settlers and, thus, more sales. The land companies deserve much of the credit for laying the foundation of permanent settlement and economy.

Prior to 1800, agriculture and commerce were the principal driving economies. After that, the Industrial Revolution began to impact all American communities, including those on the frontier. Manufacturing was on the rise, and both owners and workers demanded that the federal government protect industry from foreign imports. This sounds familiar. The Tariff of 1816 was a moderate step in that direction. Protective tariffs became a strong platform item in the future Republican Party.

Manufacturing still had a way to go throughout western Pennsylvania, but tools and other manufactured goods entering Crawford County were on the rise. It meant little to the first settlers that many of these items had come from Great Britain. Improvements in transportation and a gradual increase in the money supply enabled merchants like Frederick Haymaker and Samuel Torbett to sell the items in their Meadville stores. With more tools on store shelves, scores of artisans emerged, including carpenters, millwrights, blacksmiths, wheelwrights, tanners, spinners, etc. Brasilla Goodrich, a man who worked mechanical miracles, had a workshop of various tools that today would qualify as a hardware store. Allegedly, he made the first billiards table in Meadville, a popular attraction in town.

Obviously, the tools in 1800 lacked the fine tuning and sophistication of those manufactured a century or two later. They were basic—saws, axes, hammers—considered sufficient to build a house and barn, just enough to get started. In a short time, tool technology, availability and affordability advanced enough to spur the growth of bigger homes, stores, schools, churches, mills and roads. The mechanical side to county development from Mead's settlement in 1788 to the War of 1812, a mere two dozen years, was illustrative of the considerable progress made.

Still, that progress paled in comparison to the progress the county achieved in subsequent periods. The development years for manufacturing and tool production came with the oil boom, the railroad and the Civil War. By then, the nation and Crawford County were becoming more self-reliant industrially and less dependent upon European products. Production steadily expanded with the help of government. In 1897, Congress passed a tariff that raised duties on an average of 57 percent—making them the highest ever. Who needed European imports? We were taking care of ourselves.

The Champion Tool Company in Meadville, 1929. *Crawford County Historical Society.*

For the moment, it appeared that the initial prosperity that ushered in the twentieth century would last forever. Well, it didn't, for it never does. In the county, the blush of success in the production of tools continued in the new century with a rash of companies—1904 was a boom year. Uwanta Wrench, McNair Tool Works, G.M. Yost and Barrett Tool & Machine were among the newcomers.

Obviously, competition occurred when neighboring firms manufactured similar tools. This fact placed advertising and company slogans high on marketing agendas. For instance, McCrosky Tool, which had been McCrosky Reamer, emphasized the time- and cost-saving attributes of its tools with the slogan "Cost-cutting Tools."

Over the years, a few firms stood out among the pack. Champion Tool Company, for example, had initially existed at Conneaut Lake from 1883 to 1904. Its reputation preceded its relocation to Pine Street in Meadville. Later, the DeArments transferred the company to South Main Street. In 1963, the name of the company was changed to Channellock, nationally and internationally known for its products, including tongue-and-groove pliers.

With all its tool shops, Meadville understandably became known as the "Tool City." Elsewhere in the county there have been similar shops of equal importance, thus making tools a major segment of the county's manufacturing. Yet looking back to the earliest settlements, when neighbors often had to share a certain tool because of its scarcity or prohibitive cost, those hardworking pioneers may have wondered if one day the community might make most of the tools it needed. If it did, the pioneers would concede that the community had progressed well enough to ensure its survival.

A SALUTE TO THE
CUSTODIANS OF THE PAST

Every community has someone who can easily, and with passion, talk about the region's past. In larger communities, there are perhaps two or three such individuals. Often, they specialize in subjects they love best, such as folklore, older houses, genealogies and one-room schools. They are a fountainhead of knowledge. They advise businesses and local governments, address groups like the Boy Scouts and Kiwanians and conduct tours. And no one is better informed of the whereabouts of historical treasures than these dedicated custodians of the past. They help collect and preserve everything from letters and photographs to Civil War artifacts. Academic historians like myself, who teach and often have need for local resources, are dependent upon them. More importantly, without them, a community is in constant search of its identity.

Both local and academic historians are indebted to nineteenth-century county families—Huidekoper, Reynolds and Dick—who had a good sense of history and a deep commitment to its preservation. Many of the major manuscript collections in the county historical society were donated by these families. Not only did William Reynolds preserve and donate collections, but he wrote about the past, as well.

When I first became active with the historical society, I looked to such persons who had knowledge of their neighborhoods and were kind enough to share it. I will mention only a few who gladly helped and who are now gone. Mindful that I would surely overlook someone, I will not include any of the living who have also helped—and there have been many.

Thirty years ago, probably no one knew the western region of the county better than Emily Rankin Smith of Shermansville, Bronson Luty of Conneaut Lake and Larry Lowing of Linesville. This trio of local historians, with their storytelling, made the line between past and present seemingly melt away. And they were quick in rebuttal whenever a misstatement was either written or uttered. After remarking about an early incident at the lake, I was corrected by Emily in her caustic but harmless manner, "What do you know about that, Bob? You're a Johnny-come-lately to these parts."

I smiled and tactfully admitted, "You're right, I don't know. That's why I need your help." After that, we became the best of friends.

Emily could go through genealogical lines of local families as quickly as a ninth grader can do the alphabet. She bemoaned the passing of both the interurban trolley and, in her mind, an "entire civilization," with its cheese factories beneath the waters at Pymatuning. Witty and most cooperative, Emily was a former teacher who handled tours through the Baldwin-Reynolds House.

Luty was a historian of fine demeanor who knew Conneaut Lake, Conneaut Lake Park and its people. Railroads and trolleys were a second love of his; he could pinpoint every mile of track in the county. An engineer by profession, he enjoyed talking about the difficulties in building Route 19 through the swamp south of Meadville. At the time of his death, he possessed one of the finest photograph and postcard collections in the county. Luty spent decades meticulously preparing a memoir that was published—*The Lake As It Was* (1994)—the year after his death.

Lowing of the *Linesville Herald* spent hours with me, swapping stories on politics and the economy. Like any good newspaperman, he knew and understood people. So when I mentioned something on government, for instance, he would strengthen the story by attaching a personality or two he once knew. Larry was instrumental in organizing the historical society in Linesville and, with my urging, had a hundred years of the *Herald* microfilmed.

Another newspaperman who helped me considerably was Halver Getchell. He wrote for the *Meadville Tribune* and for years managed the historical room at the local library. I always considered him a generalist, for he knew so much about so many things, especially the story of Meadville. His articles were informative and always in good taste. He also

Halver Getchell. *Courtesy of Rebecca Getchell.*

filmed some of the construction of Interstate 79. I never could get him to tell me whether it was the bulldozer in action or the dirt being tossed that thrilled him the most. He was both a good friend and strong influence.

These four local historians had special pride in their communities. Luty filled notebooks with his memories, while Lowing and Getchell left a legacy of memorable articles. Emily Smith managed only to leave behind scattered genealogical notes. I had arranged to have her interviewed, but she died before the project was completed.

There are many local historians like Emily who never bother to publish their research. Organizations, schools and historical societies should encourage those persons to be interviewed. Oral history projects are relatively inexpensive, and interviewers can be easily trained. A number of such programs in the county have been successful; a recent one was of World War II veterans. And what is a better way to preserve the county's history and traditions than through seniors who have experienced them? I never met an elderly person who did not want to reminisce.

PRESERVING THE PAST THROUGH LOCAL HISTORY

Having recently visited Maryland, I watched a community excite itself over a research project that designated a white oak in Montgomery County as the oldest living tree in the state. The tree is anywhere from two hundred to three hundred years old and has a circumference of twenty-two feet. This reminded me of seeing the Sequoia redwoods for the first time. To this day, I'm not sure what impressed me the most, their size or age.

Regardless of where we live, most of us are intrigued by anything super old in our communities, whether it's a person, a structure or a natural phenomenon. And many of us cringe when we learn that a landmark has been bulldozed to make room for a condo or shopping mall. Under pressure from urban sprawl or the need to raise more tax dollars, governments sometimes find it expedient to use the power of eminent domain to demolish historic structures in blighted areas for new development. They call it progress.

Yet most communities I have visited are trying to preserve something of their past. Crawford County is no exception. Establishing so-called historic districts is one way that governments deal with the problem. Often, however, it is an individual or organization, like a historical society, that spearheads a drive to prevent something historically significant from being destroyed.

Our county has had, and continues to have, a number of dedicated individuals whose research brings the past to the present. Those of late who come immediately to mind include Virginia LeSueur and her original work on Meadville houses, Carl Heeschen on aesthetic architecture and Charles Jenkins on institutional archives. There were many, many others.

With today's pathfinders, I can again mention only a few. Tom Hayden and Gary Coburn continue to restore old structures. Larry Wonders is compiling a comprehensive list of some twenty-five thousand photographs held by the county historical society. Mark Roche for years has collected all things possible that deal with Cochranton's history. And Sandy Porter of Saegertown is doing what I call an "index" of bells throughout the county—predominantly church and school bells. He assures me that by the time this book goes to press he will have located nearly a hundred bells. He believes the Revere bell in the First Baptist Church in Meadville is the oldest, dating back to the 1820s or the 1830s.

All of this is local history, but its appeal is worldwide. Academic historians and other social scientists often use it to research a subject in microcosm before examining it in a wider sense. Throughout Asia and Europe, there are organizations and governments that encourage and undertake local history projects. In Finland, for example, known as *kotiseutuyo*, local history is combined with ethnology, community development and ecology and

Christmas at the Baldwin-Reynolds House. *Crawford County Historical Society.*

is practiced in the country's districts. A home district federation supports preservation, social planning and local enterprises.

In its broadest sense, local history now includes historical studies and genealogy, preservation and restoration, the environment, urban renewal, folklore and artwork. I'm sure we could expand the list. While its main attraction may be social and educational, its purposeful potential is to generate pride in one's community. And if you wonder whether there is a market twist to all this, well, there is. Local pride can often translate into dollars spent by senior tourists whose penchant to reach back in time to when life, to them, was simpler, safer and cheaper seems unlimited. I believe that tourism still ranks as one of Pennsylvania's leading industries.

Every community decides what it wants to do to help celebrate its past. Frequently, Americans are accused of not savoring our physical history as much as Europeans and Asians do. After countless centuries, there are unlimited reminders around the world of man's creative and engineering genius. It is also suggested that Americans build for the short term; many of our structures are not expected to last beyond a generation. This may be true, but in rebuttal, we can demonstrate our capacity to preserve something that may be better than any castle, wall or pyramid—namely, our national and state parks.

Preservation of paper, however, has been a nagging problem. Local history is also dependent on paper sources—public and institutional records, letters, etc. For the historian, following the paper trail is never easy. Governments and institutions are constantly ridding themselves of old stuff to make room for new stuff. To slow this destructive process, most Pennsylvania counties now have general repositories to house public and institutional archives. Public funding provides records management programs. Other counties, including Crawford, still basically rely on the institutions themselves or historical societies to maintain these records.

There are limitless ways to support local history. Subjects can vary from the simple to the more complex. Any institution or individual can initiate a project whose completion can only tell us a little more of our county's heritage. Let your local historical society know what you're researching or what you would like to undertake. Good luck.

IS OUR COUNTY A MELTING POT?

You've heard it many times: America is the country of immigrants. Each of us has an ancestor who emigrated from Europe or elsewhere on the globe. Optimists and idealists have claimed that over many generations the Americanization process has amalgamated and transformed millions of immigrants into a new national identity. Some may say the democratic spirit has caused this; others will point to the frontier, that cutting edge of civilization, as being responsible.

The term "melting pot" is a metaphor for the way a homogenous society develops. Modern sociologists have largely discarded the term, but it is still used. Calling the hypothesis a mirage, critics argue that elements in any society never fully blend. They prefer to say that society is multicultural or pluralistic—a salad bowl, so to speak.

How can the country be anything else, they ask, when classes and economic inequalities exist? Besides, they add, the immigrant has always been a problem. Labor unions and nativistic groups historically have tried, with some success, to keep people they consider to be undesirable out of the country. Congress has a long record of restrictive legislation.

So, what about Crawford County? How much of a melting pot has occurred here? That's hard to say. Many of us, perhaps most, like to believe that in recent decades the county has reached a high degree of homogeneity. We see bonding in our schools, churches, sports, workplaces, organizations and even at the county fair or the Market House. The strength of our many, many volunteers tell us that the community is working together.

Yet the critics say we are blinded by all this glitter and fail to grasp historical reality. They may have a point. The county's first settlements were disjointed and dispirited. Getting along with one's neighbors was necessary just to survive on an unforgiving frontier. The land speculator, the foreign born and the Irish were among those who were equally disliked.

Harm J. Huidekoper, a Hollander, acquired a litany of enemies for evicting squatters from Holland Land Company tracts. One of them even took a shot at "Old Harm." Fellow townsman Patrick Farrelly was hanged in effigy, and aspersions were made against his Irish ancestry simply because he stood on the wrong side of a public issue.

Huidekoper attacked both the town's "rabble" and its division. A traveler in 1816, David Thomas, alluded to Meadville's strange mix and its lack of refinement and organization. Its narrow streets, he claimed, reflected the "narrowness of its original proprietor"—David Mead. Both Thomas and Huidekoper hoped that a better brand of Easterners would come in and turn things around. Early resident John Reynolds noted how the town was so splintered that opposing groups refused to socialize.

In the 1850s, the American Party (often called the Know-Nothings) reaffirmed this diversity. Its local leaders tried to convince the electorate that the party was not against all foreigners, only those who were Catholic. Their paranoia grew from fear that Catholics were politically influenced by their priests, bishops and the pope. The party's leaders fooled no one. Their prejudice led them to nominate candidates who were white, Protestant and native born.

Our critics also faulted the Catholics. Not only did the French, Irish, Germans and Italians want their own Catholic churches, but they also sequestered themselves in separate neighborhoods. Frank Lapuma, interviewed thirty years ago, remembered these ethnic concentrations being in the "low-rent" districts of town. The nationalities generally stayed to themselves, he commented. Intermarriages were frowned upon until World War II. By then, a soldier or veteran whose family lived on South Main Street no longer hesitated to ask a young lady from upper Chestnut for a date.

Finally, the critics will use other events of the past century to prove the nonexistence of a melting pot. The flood of immigrants in the era of World War I caused nativists to cry, "Enough is enough!" They first succeeded in having a literacy requirement and then restrictive laws based on a quota system. The system favored immigrants from northern and western Europe and discriminated against those from Asia, eastern and southern Europe. The *Meadville Evening Republican* applauded these efforts and agreed with most Americans that restriction would facilitate assimilation and protect the character of the American people.

Much research work needs to be done on organizations, nationality and racial groups before any academic consensus can be reached on this question, if this is even possible. Some forty years ago, with a grant from the Ford Foundation, the Sociology Department at Allegheny College examined the black community in Meadville and concluded that serious discrimination in housing and employment still existed. Perhaps similar studies with which I'm unfamiliar have recently followed.

One recent survey of local railroad records dating back a century showed that among some fifteen hundred job applicants, thirty-nine different nationalities were represented. Many of these applicants had

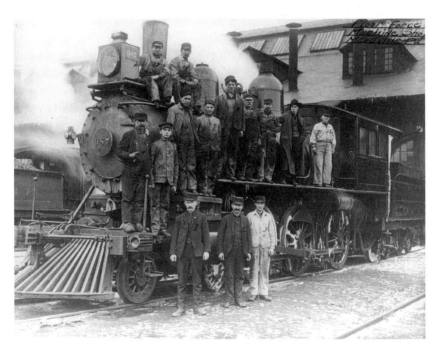

Workers at the Erie Railroad Machine Shop—a good illustration of the melting pot in the county. *Crawford County Historical Society.*

arrived after 1890, when American industry was clamoring for cheap labor and before restrictive immigration policies were adopted by the federal government. Despite their cultural differences, hundreds of men working together on the railroad gave considerable credence to the melting pot theory. The railroad yard could be an open-hearth mill or at the bottom of a mine shaft in another community.

If studies suggest that the melting pot is truly a myth, then we must look to education for help. Not so fast, our critics say. The schools only mirror society. Still, for centuries we've leaned on the schools as a fountainhead of cures for society's many ills. In 1855, the *Crawford Whig Journal* editorialized that education will end the "bitter warfare" between citizens by melting down nationality prejudices and cementing groups into "one American mold."

Schools can make a difference. What a sight it must have been in May 1921 to watch three thousand youngsters (one-fifth of the town's population) march through Meadville in defense of a bond issue for the construction of a new high school. Maybe some of you or your parents were among the marchers or viewers of this demonstration of unity. It paid off.

As a historian, I can only use available sources to describe what has happened. I must defer to my friends in sociology, anthropology and psychology to explain why things happen as they do when different cultures come face to face. I'll ask them if they think an "American mold" has emerged in the county, or do we simply feel it has because we all speak "American."

And if language is the standard, then the county is ahead of the nation. A recent survey shows that out of 1,000 residents, 173 speak a foreign language at home.

SOCIETY CELEBRATES A
CENTURY OF PROGRESS

On October 8, 1980, more than a hundred people helped the Crawford County Historical Society celebrate its centennial with a program of lectures and exhibits. The general theme was the progress in the society's first century. Robert S. Bates, former president of the society, spoke on the early history of the organization; Librarian Robert D. Ilisevich discussed the society's archives; and a member of the society's board of directors, Louise Sturdevant, reported on the acquisition of the Baldwin-Reynolds House and the Dr. J. Russell Mosier office building.

Having a historical organization was the dream of many nineteenth-century county residents. According to Bates, the Meadville community, almost from its founding, had a "broad commitment to things of the intellect." Citizens placed a high value upon their own worth as individuals and upon the institutions of their community and nation. They had a sense of social responsibility and historical preservation. Although the Civil War gave to the people a considerable amount of national pride, it also encouraged them to take greater interest in their own local history. After the war, anything cultural was given a boost. Prominent businessmen, like Huidekoper, Reynolds and Dicks, promoted and supported the organization of schools, libraries and professional societies—scientific, literary and historical.

"A common interest in art and history, as well as literature," Bates went on, "prompted a group of culturally oriented civic leaders to organize the Meadville Library, Art and Historical Association on May 10, 1879, for the purpose of consolidating their varied interests in one organization."

Robert S. Bates. *Crawford County Historical Society.*

Shortly thereafter, the association purchased the Huidekoper woolen mill on Park Avenue and Center Street, the present site of the Mercatoris Building. The historical rooms within "Library Hall," as the building was called, served as the depository for collected records of the early history of the county and state. These included letters, papers and journals of first settlers, maps, newspapers, oil portraits and artifacts from local mounds of the earliest Indian cultures.

The building was the birthplace of the historical society as an independent organization. The date: February 16, 1880. It sponsored monthly lectures and readings for the public during subsequent years. Its first major activity was to promote the observance of the Meadville centennial, and it did so in grand fashion. The *Daily Tribune-Republican* published a special centennial edition composed of numerous historical essays authored by a number of local citizens. After this successful celebration, interest dwindled, and for almost fifty years, the organization remained virtually dormant.

In 1935, under the leadership of John Earle Reynolds, the society was resurrected in its new home on the corner of North Main and Walnut Streets, where it had moved nine years earlier. Interest in the organization increased as the 150th birthday of Meadville approached. At a November meeting in that year, Robert S. Bates became the president of the newly revived society. Under his direction, the historical collections were sorted and organized, while a number of things were put on display. A special committee began work on plans for the sesquicentennial celebration of 1938, which turned out to be a memorable event for the community. The *Tribune-Republican* prepared for the occasion its special "Sesquicentennial Edition," while John E. Reynolds wrote a short but fascinating history entitled *In French Creek Valley*. Proceeds from the sale of this book went to the benefit of the society.

According to Bates,

> *Interest in local history reached such a peak during the celebration that at its conclusion no one contemplated the possibility of closing up shop and putting the historical society in mothballs, as had happened after the 1888 celebration. Instead, the collection was enlarged by a tremendous number of significant acquisitions, and interesting programs were presented at society meetings.*

Since then, the society has remained active. Dedicated people, additional staff and modern facilities have increased public involvement. The number of donations in the past forty years have been impressive, thus making the archival collection one of the finest of any society of equal size. As Librarian Ilisevich pointed out, it is what the society library has to offer in the way of research materials and services that attracts visitors. He noted that the current collection now includes, in addition to many books, maps, photographs and stereographs, local newspapers dating back to 1805; the federal census; cemetery lists; high school and Allegheny College yearbooks; city and county directories; tax assessment ledgers; a vertical file of assorted information on assorted subjects; genealogies; paintings by local artists; and thousands of letters and papers, account books, memoirs and diaries that, together, make up the manuscript collection.

Money has been a problem for the society from the very beginning, but recently government and private funding has eased some of the financial burden. Appropriations from the county commissioners have increased, and donations have led to an endowment program. This past year, the society received a grant from the Harry C. Winslow Foundation to continue microfilming old newspapers. Government funds under the CETA program have given the society critically needed personnel over the last five years. The most recent addition is the county investigator of archival materials. His project, the first of its kind in Pennsylvania, involves the survey of the county to determine the existence of any documentary sources held by institutions that may have historical significance.

Other major undertakings of the society during the past several decades have been the acquisition of the Baldwin-Reynolds House on Terrace Street and the Dr. J. Russell Mosier office building of Littles Corners. In 1963, after the death of Katherine Reynolds, the Baldwin-Reynolds House was offered to the society at a price considerably lower than its estimated market value. Through a public fund drive, the society raised the necessary monies to purchase the home. With the help of a volunteer staff and one part-time paid employee, the mansion is maintained as a period house and museum. From May through September, public tours are given.

The Mosier property came to the society through Edward Mosier, the grandson of Dr. Mosier. He felt that the building and its contents should be retained in the county and preserved as a historical site. Virtually untouched for nearly forty years, the doctor having died in 1938, the tiny office building is a memorial to the country doctor of yesteryear. Again, through a responsive public, the society collected approximately $10,000 for the removal and restoration of the building. On November 21, 1975, the building was moved to its present site on the Baldwin-Reynolds property. Both the house and the physician's office are listed on the National Register of Historic Places.

The evening celebration climaxed with special awards. Halver Getchell received an inscribed brass plaque for his years of dedicated service in the society's development and for his help in the acquisition of the Baldwin-Reynolds House. For her unique contribution in researching and writing *Placing Bits and Pieces of Meadville's Hundred Years*, Virginia LeSueur received a deluxe edition of *In French Creek Valley* by John Reynolds. Finally, a brass plaque was awarded to Robert S. Bates for his distinctive service in the reorganization of the society and for his consistent support for more than forty-five years.

The centennial celebration was a review of the society's history and accomplishments of the past one hundred years, but it was also an expression of hope for the continued progress in the next century.

BLACKOUTS? EARTH HOUR? PLEASE, JUST TURN OFF THE LIGHTS

Recently, hundreds of cities in the United States and across the globe participated in Earth Hour by turning off their lights for one hour "in support for action on climate change." It is hoped that other cities and communities will do something similar in the future.

Pittsburgh was one of the participating cities. Turning off the lights reminded me of the blackouts I experienced in this industrial city during the "Big One" (World War II). Certainly, those blackouts were not designed to reduce carbon emission, but to prepare the public for possible enemy air strikes. Smog-smitten Pittsburghers were accustomed to enduring many autumn and winter days when the sun disappeared between dawn and dusk. Streetlights remained on all day, while concerned parents, afraid their children might get lost in the dark, walked them to and from school. Unnerving neither my parents nor their neighbors, these blackouts merely added another dimension to the state of being in the dark.

During the war, Meadville and Crawford County also had blackouts and air-raid drills. The area was in the Pittsburgh defense region with such potential targets as Talon, Viscose, Keystone Ordnance Works and the Erie Railroad with its shops. The commander of the Crawford County Citizens Defense Corps, Donald C. Thompson, warned: "We in Meadville are in strategic danger of air raids…because we are in a direct line between the ore-carrying Great Lakes canals and steel-producing Pittsburgh." The warning sparked the community to organize for emergency preparedness.

Meadville had four air-raid districts, with many hundreds of volunteer wardens. There were "partial" and "total" blackouts. A partial ran from dusk to dawn; a total lasted for a half hour and was generally announced by a siren. The army stipulated regulations for air-raid drills and had them published in the local newspaper. Also listed were games that could be played in the dark; that is, children's games. The volunteers walked the streets to see that residents took these drills seriously. After one such drill in July 1942, nearly two dozen violators were charged, and those found guilty paid a fine of $27.50, a hefty amount in those days.

In November of that year, Frank W. Gapp, staff writer for the *Tribune-Republican*, simulated a crisis in the city following an air assault. In a three-pronged attack against Pittsburgh, Buffalo and Meadville, a number of new German Heinkel bombers, each with a payload of two tons of explosives, broke through American defenses. Many were shot down. Unable to make the long return trip, the surviving planes eventually had to land in the United States or Canada. Germany considered the loss of all those men and planes justified if some American production was halted. Those bombers that reached Crawford County did heavy damage to Meadville, Gapp reported. Talon was hit hard, with fifteen workers killed and many more seriously hurt. Incinerating bombs touched off numerous fires. Both hospitals were filled with emergency cases, and schools were temporarily converted into first-aid stations.

Fortunately, none of this actually happened. But an awareness of what could happen intensified, for in 1942, Germany was still the nation with the strongest military force on Earth. Its Panzer divisions were moving closer to Moscow, Leningrad and the Suez Canal. In addition, its industrial output remained basically intact, while its scientists busied themselves inventing crazy military hardware. Despite its air defeat in the Battle of Britain, Germany, in 1942, had to be taken seriously, and so did emergency preparedness.

Reportedly, the area had one of the better civil defense organizations—under the guidance of the Crawford County Defense Council and the Meadville Defense Council. Citizen mobilization was remarkable. On February 21, 1942, some fourteen hundred civil defense volunteers paraded before several thousand chilled spectators who braved snow and ten-degree temperatures to show their appreciation. It was a demonstration of one group of civilians honoring another group of civilians, a testament

A World War II bond parade in Meadville. This was just one of the many rallies during the war. *Crawford County Historical Society.*

to the kind of patriotic unity that prevailed on the homefront. We have not seen this kind of support in all of our other wars.

Those who remember the blackouts naturally recall personal events—hurrying to the store for candles before the next drill, gathering with family in a basement that had no windows and getting the children ready for bed before it got dark in the event of a drill. Lucille Albaugh still remembers the window behind the altar in St. Agatha's Church being covered to prevent a sliver of light from escaping. People did what they had to do. One octogenarian harboring some tragic memories, however, remarked that she didn't wish to recall anything of the war.

It may be a mean stretch to find a close relationship between blackouts and Earth Hour. While the latter looks for ways to save the planet, the former reflects a nation's past determination to save a little of itself. Aside from the community spirit, a hidden element in both is conservation. Never were blackouts intended to save on electricity, though communities did save many kilowatts by having lights dimmed or turned off. Earth Hour simply implies how carbon emission can be reduced by cutting back on electricity.

Saving energy today does not seem to be a strong incentive for most Americans. Motivation to conserve may increase as energy supplies lessen and costs rise. In our two major wars of the past century, conservation, and even the rationing of consumer goods in World War II, went toward easing national waste. For a political candidate to recommend rationing of any kind today would be a kiss of death to his candidacy.

Still, I remember our air-raid warden always saying, "Please turn off your light and you'll save on your electric bill."

CONNEAUT LAKE IS A WESTERN PARADISE

Conneaut Lake was most familiar to Native Americans. The word "conneaut" most likely is derived from the Seneca term for "snow." Many of David Mead's settlers, including Cornelius Van Horne, did not know at first that such a body of water existed. Abner Evans changed all this in the 1790s, when he settled at the foot of the lake.

Both settlement and activities increased. The French Creek Feeder Canal ushered in an era of high hopes for individuals who saw the raw potential of the area. The lake was elevated with water from French Creek to accommodate boats towed either toward Erie or the Beaver Valley on the Beaver and Lake Erie Canal. Despite its immense popularity in Pennsylvania and neighboring states, the canal was too slow and too easily victimized by the weather. Once the railroad arrived, the days of the canal were numbered.

The railroad revolutionized the way people lived and how businesses operated. When the Atlantic and Great Western Railroad finally made its way to Meadville during the Civil War, land values along its path went up. Naturally, Evansburg (now Conneaut Lake) benefited, as did other communities. Thomas Kennard, the engineer mainly responsible for the construction of the A&GW, sought property investment around the lake, as did many others.

A reasonable argument can be made that, had it not been for the railroad, Conneaut Lake's growth and popularity would not have occurred. It was not uncommon many years ago to see, on a given day, well over a thousand people brought to Exposition Park at the lake by trains from Pittsburgh and Cleveland. A working relationship resulted between the lake's enterprises and railroads like the Pittsburgh, Shenango and Lake Erie Railroad, the Meadville and Linesville Railroad and the Pittsburgh, Bessemer and Lake Erie Railroad.

In addition to the trains, there was the trolley or interurban car. While generally associated with large urban areas, the interurban also connected and benefited small towns as long as there were tracks laid, a power plant installed and electrical lines stretched. Most cars were ordinary, comfortable and safe. Of course, there were accidents as there are with every form of travel. Some cars were luxurious, with observation platforms, stained glass and washrooms. A few even had sleeping accommodations.

In the 1890s, the Meadville Street Railway Company was offered a franchise to run a line beyond the city limits. For the next few years, the line ran a short distance, but in 1906 construction began along Cussewago Road for the Meadville and Conneaut Lake Traction Company. The track reached Harmonsburg the next spring and Exposition Park that summer.

A trolley wreck on the Harmonsburg Line. Accidents on the interurban line were not frequent, but they did occur. *Crawford County Historical Society.*

The interurban enjoyed a distinct advantage over the train. It could maneuver the hills better. There was some steep grading on the Harmonsburg Pike, but it was not an impossible problem. From Harmonsburg to Linesville, the ground was practically level. Outside Harmonsburg, the trolley track had to cross over the Bessemer Railroad track on a bridge that had to be built. This construction slowed the laying of track toward Linesville.

For several decades, the interurban retained public support, but like every preceding system of transportation—stagecoach, canal, railroad—it met a challenge from a newcomer. This time it was the motor car.

Regardless of the mode of travel, visitors went to the lake. Before Exposition Park, they enjoyed themselves at the Oakland Beach picnic grove or by cruising on a steam pleasure boat or sailing yacht. Some of the steamboats were the *Queen*, *Tuna*, *Keystone* and the *Nickel Plate*. The last mentioned was a double-decker and, at the time, the largest boat on the lake. There were countless others simply because there was nothing as romantic or relaxing as a cruise around the lake. Boating and picnicking

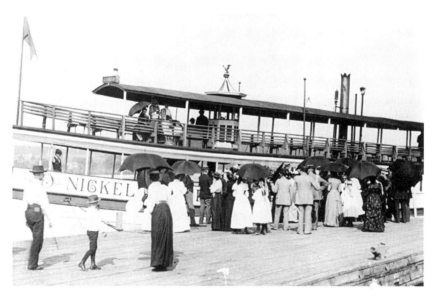

The *Nickel Plate* steamship on Conneaut Lake—one of many, many vessels on the lake. *Crawford County Historical Society.*

seemed satisfying enough for most visitors, but for one man it was not enough. He wanted to broaden the entertainment base to please other groups, particularly farmers and professionals.

Frank Mantor was a person of rare abilities and pursuits. Born near Conneautville, he attended local academies and afterward worked a short time in the mercantile business. When he gave that up, he turned to politics. With J.W. Patten of Conneautville and Alfred Huidekoper of Meadville, Mantor helped organize the Republican Party of western Pennsylvania. After the Civil War, he served in the state senate and held a clerkship in the administration of Governor James Beaver. Bored with government service, he resigned in 1892 to promote a project very dear to him—an exposition park of a particular kind at Conneaut Lake—for which he is best remembered.

It was an age of Chautauquas, amusement and exposition parks. In Crawford County, Perkins Park in Cambridge Springs and Oakwood Park in Meadville were good examples. They were small, but most appealing to local residents. Apparently, Mantor's park plan occurred to him after he had visited the famous Williams Grove Association, south of Harrisburg.

Mantor wanted to create something that would combine an annual exhibit of products, stock and machinery from the region with the Chautauqua idea that provided an educational and entertaining assembly of concert performers and leading lecturers. He also hoped to have a summer school for teachers to help broaden their horizons. The stock exhibit was to rely upon the stock farms of Miller and Sibley of Franklin, the Powell Brothers of Shadeland and A.C. Huidekoper's Little Missouri Stock Farm in Conneaut Lake.

Mantor's grandiose plan impressed a number of business and civic leaders. In April 1892, a group of them organized the "Conneaut Lake Exposition Company" with capitalization fixed at $25,000. The incorporation included A.C. Huidekoper, Samuel B. Dick, S.H. Wilson and Frank Mantor, who became superintendent. The company bought John McClure's farm and the Lynce Landing properties on the west side of the lake. Among the scheduled facilities were a five-thousand- to ten-thousand-seat auditorium and a hotel. In time, a ball field was added with a quarter-mile racetrack.

The immediate success of the park did not exactly reflect Mantor's exposition/Chautauqua ideal. Yet it became a wonderful getaway—one

Exposition Park. *Crawford County Historical Society.*

of the best known in the state. Church groups and other organizations, like the Granges, loved to use it for their gatherings and conventions. Over the years, temperance, labor and political speakers have excited audiences in the spacious auditorium, as have musical groups.

Before World War I, one form of entertainment enjoyed by all were the aerial maneuvers by barnstorming aviators. This was the time of the "stick-and-wire" flying machines. One of the first pilots to demonstrate his skills at the lake was Paul Peck, who performed in the summer of 1911. Doing fancy aerobatics at eight hundred feet kept the spectators spellbound until, one day, he crash-landed. Thankfully, he escaped injury. Another performer was L. Earle Sandt of nearby Brookville. Prior to his engagement at the lake in 1912, he had gained national attention with his fearless flight across Lake Erie in winter. He also crashed at Conneaut Lake and suffered broken ribs. His luck ran out at Grove City, where he died following an accident.

The science and marvels of flight, either in a plane or balloon, fascinated most Americans. Early aviators knew this and hoped to capitalize on it by teaching others to fly. Some opened schools and started a craze that became nationwide. The famous Wright brothers began the first school in 1909 in Dayton, Ohio. Six years later, Ernest C. Hall opened his flying school at Exposition Park. One magazine advertised that vacationers could learn to fly in a perfectly safe 135-horsepower seaplane. Hall charged $90 per hour, or $400 for the complete course, which could include room and board! (You can do the math and figure what this means in today's dollars.) Odd as it may seem, however, a local newspaper reported that the flights were popular, and Hall's service was in demand.

Frank Mantor did not live long enough to witness the evolution of Conneaut Lake Park, for he died in 1895. The variety of rides, a sandy beach, a large picnic area and a ballroom probably crossed his mind, for he knew what was happening at vacation parks. Had he lived into the twentieth century, it is not unreasonable to presume that he would have accepted the course the park eventually took. Although he was an idealist, a man of convictions, he was also a progressive, quick to adapt to changing situations, as his entire career suggests.

Conneaut Lake has had a remarkable history. Many will always remember it as a fun place—boating, sailing, amusement rides, holiday fireworks, Dreamland Ballroom. When I asked a former colleague of mine from Pittsburgh how he and his family enjoyed their vacation in the western part of the county and at the lake, he said it best: "Conneaut Lake is a western paradise."

ABOUT THE AUTHOR

Robert D. Ilisevich, a native of Pittsburgh, did his undergraduate and graduate work at the University of Pittsburgh and Western Reserve University in Cleveland. He completed thirty-four years of teaching American history at the university and college levels, finishing his career at Mercyhurst College, Erie.

He has authored and co-edited a half dozen books on Pennsylvania history and biography, with most of them on the northwestern region of the commonwealth. His articles have appeared in newspapers and in international, national and state historical journals. For more than a dozen years, he was librarian/archivist of the Crawford County Historical Society and editor of its newsletter.

He lives with his wife, Agnes, in Meadville, Pennsylvania.

Visit us at
www.historypress.net